A HIGH SCHOOL
WORK-STUDY PROGRAM
FOR MENTALLY
SUBNORMAL STUDENTS

A **HIGH SCHOOL WORK-STUDY PROGRAM** FOR MENTALLY **SUBNORMAL STUDENTS**

Oliver P. Kolstoe
AND
Roger M. Frey

SOUTHERN ILLINOIS UNIVERSITY PRESS
Carbondale and Edwardsville

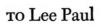

TO Lee Paul

PREFACE

THE AUTHORS' accumulated experience of service, research, and teaching the mentally retarded in public schools, clinics, institutions, residential facilities, and sheltered work programs, prompted the writing of this book. The book itself is a distillation of those experiences which represent the most fruitful of the practices encountered. The rapidly expanding body of research in this area is not presented. The authors have deliberately avoided an extensive review of research since this is available from other sources. They have instead selected those studies they found most pertinent to the understanding of the program presented in this book.

The inclusion of bibliographical references has made it possible for the authors to concentrate their attention on details which would seem to be of most use to school personnel. The book, therefore, pays considerable attention to a rationale which may be of use to administrators and school board members who wish to inform their constituents of the need and the reasons for programs. The major content of the book is intended primarily for teachers and work-study supervisors. Although various curricular arrangements could have been used, the authors considered the development of academic and vocational skills which move through successive levels of complexity to be the most suitable warp through which the vertical threads of personal and social development could be woven to form a program fabric.

Although the high school program is presented as a four-year experience, there is no intention on the part of the authors to imply that each youngster should follow the set program in a lock-step manner. Indeed, to do justice to individual differences, the authors suggest that the program sequence be violated as the needs of the youngsters suggest specific modification. The program is presented as something that can be departed from in the best interests of an individual student.

Throughout the eight years which were invested in the development of this book, many individuals provided noteworthy help, both material and spiritual. Thanks are given to Robert M. Tomlinson, Don and Bette Baldis, Dick and Mary Bufkin, and Vince and Pat Farrell, who served, at various times, as directors of the Employment Training Center of Southern Illinois University. Special thanks are due our colleagues Charles E. Skinner, Juilus Cohen, Guy Renzaglia, Thomas E. Jordan, Dan S. Rainey, Elizabeth McKay, and R. Murray Chastain for their willingness to read, criticize, and edit the manuscript. Perhaps most important is the contribution of the administrators and the school boards of the Kent County, Michigan, Special Education District and the Carbondale Community High School District who allowed Fount Warren and Richard Smith to try experimental work-study programs which give the manuscript the authority which comes from the test of use.

Oliver P. Kolstoe
Roger M. Frey

January 20, 1965

CONTENTS

A HIGH SCHOOL
WORK-STUDY PROGRAM
FOR MENTALLY
SUBNORMAL STUDENTS

1

HISTORY

Early provisions for the disabled

CONCERN about people who are disabled has never been so great as it is at the present time. This concern is not new but the treatment accorded the disabled has changed radically throughout history. Whether fortunately or unfortunately, the popular attitude toward the disabled has dictated the kind of treatment which the disabled have received.

While political philosophy is often thought of as distinct from educational philosophy, the close relationship between political philosophy and treatment of the disabled seems inescapable. At one extreme is the concern for the welfare of the state as exemplified by Marxism.

Probably the earliest example of political philosophy as it affects the disabled is provided by the Greeks. Among the early Greeks, and especially among the Spartans, where the concern of the populace was to develop a citizenry free of defective people, crippled individuals were left out in the hills to perish. This system of eliminating disabled individuals could well be called the "era of extermination." It should be noted that the reason for the type of treatment which was accorded the disabled was primarily based on the militaristic attitude of the Spartans and their desire to have a population suited to the harsh demands of military service. Inherent in this kind of treatment is the implicit assumption that an individual is what he is, now and forever. That people should receive differential treatment according to their contribution to the welfare of the state seemed to be an unquestioned premise.

During the Middle Ages as small independent kingdoms were beginning to develop in Europe, the treatment of the disabled changed in accordance with the needs of the culture. In return for protection, the peasants served the newly-established nobles through a complex system of labor and taxation. Service might include working the lands of the noble, fighting in his army, or according him special privileges which would make his life somewhat more interesting or comfortable. It was during this time that disabled individuals were often provided a measure of safety by the noble, and in return they acted as jesters or simply allowed themselves to be ridiculed for their deformities or foolish behavior. This system of caring for the disabled may be termed an "era of ridicule." It should be obvious that making fun of the disabled or laughing at them fulfilled a great need, for this society had to find ways of discriminating between individuals as the basis of a developing, rigid, caste system. Despite the savage ridicule, the era was a step toward the humanitarian treatment of disabled people; it certainly was an improvement over systematic extermination. Yet it was fundamentally not different from extermination in a philosophical sense.

With the beginning of the Renaissance, the Roman Catholic church set the mode of behavior for the handling of the disabled by accepting them as wards of the church and caring for them in monasteries or asylums. Because of this institutional care, this period could be known as the "era of asylum." Their motives for providing an asylum for the disabled are not completely clear, but it seems evident that the doctrine of Christianity which preached that all human beings are children of God and therefore precious in His sight would indicate that all individuals should be given humane treatment. To the degree that they were helpless or childlike, it became expedient to provide for protection either in the monastery or a specialized institution. The "era of asylum" marked a giant stride forward in the treatment of the disabled; a vast improvement over either extermination or ridicule. Yet this was also akin to extermination in that the disabled were removed from society in general.

It is quite evident that the development of a social conscience among the stabilized countries was making a beginning. Attempts to distinguish between the deserving and the undeserving poor is apparent in the passage of poor laws in the Middle Ages. Even the alms houses were originally designed to help the unfortunate to help themselves. That this had a profound effect on the treatment of the disabled seems undeniable.

Perhaps the happiest circumstance, however, occurred in the monasteries. Since most of the monks were educated people, and since many of the asylums or institutions were run by the church-affiliated groups, it was inevitable that over a period of time many of the monks would attempt to extend education to their wards. This became most evident during the early part of the eighteenth century prior to the Industrial Revolution. The educational program was confined primarily to work within institutions. Nevertheless, this set the pattern for educational programs in public and private schools which developed in Europe, in England, and in the United States during this period. It is this educational movement which has brought about the "era of education" in the care of the disabled.

As was true in the other eras, it is difficult to pinpoint the precise motives which may have been operating. Nevertheless, it seems quite evident that the Industrial Revolution and the need for mass education for the development of a literate people had its effect on the educational programs for the disabled. Philosophically, this was a fundamental shift in belief as to the nature of man—a demonstration of faith in the modifiability of man's behavior through education.

The extension and improvement of education for the disabled has continued to the present day, and during the latter part of the 1940's and early 1950's a definite trend in the educational programs for all disabled individuals is discernible. The literature notes increased attempts to provide for the vocational independence and has led to the identification of a new era in the treatment of the disabled: namely, an "occupational adequacy era." The growth of sheltered workshops, work placement programs within and outside of institutions, public school programs for the mentally disabled, has been marked during the 1950's and 1960's. Thus the program of education for education's sake has given way to specific goals; i.e., the occupational adequacy of each disabled individual to facilitate his personal and social development.

It is evident that the concern for the welfare of the disabled has always been dictated by the needs of society. In the complexity of our modern civilization, the need for well-trained and well-informed people who can contribute their share to the general welfare of the nation has become greater and greater. Perhaps never in history have we had welfare programs as consistent and effective as those which exist at the present time. The goals of these welfare programs are changing. Formerly these programs provided a dole or, at best, unspecialized care; they now provide for the habilitation or rehabilitation of individuals who then can become independent, productive members of our society. Here again societal needs have dictated the direction which concern for the disabled will take.

It is difficult to assess what degree the concern for the development of every individual recognizes the assumption that man is capable of improvement or change through experience. Yet underlying the philosophical patterns which condoned the destruction of the unwanted to the elaborate contemporary programs of training are all shades of opinion concerning the immutable nature of man. Modern western thought holds philosophically to the concept of the modifiable nature of man. Coupled to this is the political doctrine of the western world that government by consent of the governed requires the fullest development of the abilities of each individual. The implementation of this position through the medium of mass education brings squarely into focus the nature-nurture problem. How much of man's behavior is genetically determined, and how much is determined by experience? It is obvious that this question is unresolved and that modern western society is not unanimous in its philosophical commitment.

It is easy to identify practices held over from former eras. It is not unusual even today to read of instances where parents have destroyed their disabled children. The stereotype of the village idiot is evidence of the persistence of the "era of ridicule." Even though education and vocational programs have grown enormously in the past few years, waiting periods for admission to institutions intended especially for the mentally retarded may be as long as two or three years; evidence of the persistence of the "era of asylum." At the same time, it is not at all unusual to find educational programs for the mentally retarded which are just simplified versions of the education provided for normal children in the regular classroom and which have few if any of the elements of vocational training.

Some hope for a better understanding of the nature-nurture question may come from attempts which have been made to explain individual differences in mental ability: in short, from definitions of mental retardation.

Definitions of mental retardation
Mental retardation as a developmental defect

Itard (1800)[1] should probably be given credit for the first really systematic effort to educate the mentally retarded. A sensationist, after the pattern of Locke, Itard believed that the intellectual level at which any individual might function was largely a product of the kinds of environmental influences which the individual had been exposed to during his development.

In 1799 Itard had the opportunity to work with a boy who had been found running wild in the woods of Aveyron, France. This wild boy, whom Itard named Victor, was animal-like in all of his behavior. Itard apparently reasoned that the animal-like behavior of Victor was a product of his having grown up in the woods where his environmental influences were primarily those to which animals were exposed. Believing that he could civilize Victor by presenting him with sensory stimulations of a civilized variety, Itard spent the next few years in a sense-training program with Victor. For example, Itard attempted to teach the sense discrimination of hot and cold to Victor; presumably not to make him aware of hotness and coldness as such, but rather to make him sufficiently aware of temperature changes that he might dress in an appropriate manner and thus appear more human and less like an animal. Although Itard believed the experiment ended in failure, it set the pattern for a sense-training program and provided a basis for speculation as to the role of heredity versus environment in the growth and final functioning level of an individual. Furthermore, this was the first suggestion that subnormal and subhuman behavior may be a developmental defect: the results of environmental inadequacies as they contribute to the development of an individual. In a sense this constitutes the first definition of what mental retardation may be and also what causes mental retardation in the first place.

The work of Itard was followed by that of his student Seguin.[2] Seguin was considerably more generous in his appraisal of the success of Itard's work than was Itard himself. Nevertheless, he departed from the original definition of mental retardation as an environmentally controlled developmental defect, reasoning that the developmental defect was caused by the faulty transmission of sensations from the environment of the individual to his nervous system. That is, Seguin speculated that the lack of development was related to defects in the nervous system. Sensory stimulation from the environment failed to get to the brain of the individual. Therefore, the person failed to develop not because of the kinds of stimuli to which he had been exposed, but rather because the organic defect in the nervous system made it impossible for responses to sensory stimuli to be retained or learned. Although the developmental deficiency definition of mental retardation was, in a sense, continued by Seguin, his was a clear-cut definition of an *organic* cause of mental retardation rather than a strictly *environmental* one.

Mental retardation as a psychological defect

Although the definition of mental retardation as a developmental defect arising from the sensory deprivation of environment and an organic defect was a significant beginning, no very great progress toward defining mental retardation was made until Alfred Binet and Theodore Simon[3] were commissioned by the officials of Paris to construct a test which would identify the Paris school children who could not profit from education. Faced with the formidable task of really defining what was meant by intelligence (and by implication, what was meant by mental retardation), Binet and Simon first tried to separate intellectual functions into related units of behavior. This well-documented work is described by Cronbach,[4] Dennis,[5] and others.

It is interesting to note that Binet and Simon tried to find a relationship between intelligence and such things as reaction time, palmistry, finger length, space between the eyes, phrenology, and handwriting. It is significant, however, that no real progress took place until they abandoned the attempts to describe what intelligence is and concentrated instead on trying to discover what people who are intelligent can do that unintelligent persons cannot.

Binet and Simon devised a series of tasks which called for the exercise of memory, solving puzzles, finding likenesses and differences, detecting absurdities, formulating plans, and abstracting ideas. It may be noted that these were considerably more complex in functioning than the simple sensory tools that absorbed their attention primarily. These tasks were given to many children of various ages. Then the per cent of children at each age level who successfully performed each task was carefully plotted on a graph. Any task which was successfully performed by approximately 50 per cent of the children of a given age was judged to be appropriate for that age level. Binet and Simon then arranged the tasks into the proper age groups, and the first workable test of intelligence was born. It was now possible to compare the mental performance of any child with other children of the same chronological age. A bright child can not only perform those tasks at his chronological level but also some tasks at a higher age level. A mentally retarded child can perform only the tasks of younger aged children. Binet went on to develop what has come to be called the Mental Age Scale: a series of mental tasks appropriate to the performance of normal children of successively higher age levels.

In effect Binet and Simon actually defined intelligence by the type of items they included in their scale. William Stern[6] pointed out that the *level* of mental development could be converted into a *rate* of mental development by dividing the child's mental age by his chronological age. This results in the intelligence quotient or I.Q.: the highly useful index for expressing a child's *rate* of mental development.

In 1870, a Lunacy Act was passed by the British Parliament. This act defined conditions of mental illness and provided for the humane treatment and care of those individuals. Unfortunately, it was not until the Binet-Simon Scale was made available around 1904 that a very clear distinction between mental retardation and mental illness could be detected. With this instrument, the British Royal Commission for the Feeble-Minded made its report which was enacted into law in 1908. Their chief task was to recommend a method of distinguishing between those patients who were mentally ill and those who were mentally retarded, so that appropriate treatments could be instituted for each group. Probably taking their cue from the developmental defect line of reasoning, they described mental retardation in terms of the level of social behavior of which a mentally retarded adult may be capable. By associating these behavior descriptions with the I.Q. and also the mental age, they arrived at a description of the expected adult behaviors for various levels of mental retardation.

These levels of retardation are as follows:

1] An *idiot* is a mentally retarded individual with an I.Q. of below 25 and who even as an adult is incapable of learning the rudiments of school work. He is not capable of taking care of his personal needs and cannot protect himself from the ordinary hazards of living. In most instances he requires supervision and external support for his protection and also for his survival.

2] An *imbecile* is one whose I.Q. is between 25 and 50. Although able to express his wants verbally, to care for himself personally and to do work under conditions of adequate supervision and support, he requires supervision and at least partial support for his existence. The academic expectations of an imbecile are approximately that of a normal child of age five or six.

3] A *feeble-minded* person is defined as an individual whose I.Q. ranges upward from 50 to approximately 70. His mental age at adulthood is between 7 and 9, and he would be capable of academic achievement typical of a third or fourth grade level in school. Under favorable circumstances and with training, the feeble-minded could be expected to become partially or fully self-supporting and work with little or no supervision at tasks which do not require a great deal of judgment or foresight. Typically these individuals could be expected to work in a satisfactory manner, but they would be apt, because of their lack of foresight and judgment, to do things which might be considered "foolish."

This description of mental retardation in terms of I.Q., mental age, and inadequate social behavior provided a definition of mental retardation. As a result of the Commission's report, mental retardation was described not only in terms of the expected inadequate adult behavior, but levels of retardation were delineated, named, and described. The terms *feeble-minded, imbecile,* and *idiot* became a legitimate part of the clinical vocabulary: useful for describing the degree of developmental defect as well as providing a frame of reference for planning purposes.

Many decades of work and experimentation have gone by since the Binet-Simon Scale and the British Royal Commission Classification System appeared in the United States. Hundreds of intelligence tests have been offered by test constructors. While the procedure, method of scoring, and items included may be quite different from the original Binet-Simon Scale (and even the various revisions of the Binet done by Dr. Lewis Terman[7] and his students at Stanford University), all the tests have in common the comparison of the mental performance of one child with other children of the similar age and cultural background, and the classification of children by levels of performance. From these tests it is not only possible to identify a child who is mentally retarded, but it is possible to determine relatively the degree of retardation and the intellectual areas in which he is most efficient. Furthermore, the I.Q. makes it possible to identify the mentally retarded while they are children. It is no longer necessary to wait until a person exhibits inadequate social behavior as an adult as was necessary when using the criterion of inadequate social behavior suggested by the British Royal Commission.

This psychological method for identifying and classifying children who are mentally retarded was a great boon to workers in the field. While it is unfortunate that the very usefulness of the tests has also contributed to their overuse and abuse by naive and zealous practitioners, inadequate test performance still remains the standard method of identifying and defining what is meant by mental retardation. It has added a great deal of precision in the distinguishing between what is mental illness and what is inadequate behavior which results from inadequate mental development.

Mental retardation as a medical defect

Since all degrees of mental retardation exist and with such a variety of accompanying conditions, it is inevitable that along with the description of inadequate social behavior and subnormal psychological test performance would come other kinds of descriptions and classifications. In 1866 Down[8] described the physical characteristics of the condition called *mongolism*. He included in the description the information that youngsters with this condition were generally found to have intellectual characteristics no higher than those of idiots and imbeciles. Since that time, other medical workers have attempted to inject some medical aspects into the general description of mental retardation. Jervis[9] defined mental deficiency in the following manner: "Mental deficiency may be defined, from a medical point of view, as a condition of arrest or incomplete mental development induced by disease or injury before adolescence or arising from genetic cause." This description, which was published in 1952, is characteristic of other medical definitions in that they attempt to explain the causes, or etiology, of mental retardation. Strauss and Lehtinen,[10] and Strauss and Kephart[11] (for instance) classified mental retardation according to causes into either endogenous or exogenous categories. Endogenous mental retardation was presumed to arise from causes which were inherently within the individual. The exogenous type of mental retardation was described as that which was caused by conditions outside of the individual such as a disease, brain damage, or some other trauma.

Implicit in the medical definitions is the assumption that mental retardation results from an insult to the mental equipment of the person. At base, it is assumed that some physical insult to the organism is responsible for the retardation and that the damage is of a permanent type; so much so that the future functioning is forever altered. Their alignment is clearly on the side of "nature" in the "nature-nurture" controversy.

Mental retardation as an educational defect

As problems having to do with training have become important, it has seemed necessary to define mental retardation in terms which might provide some clues for training. Kirk and Johnson[12] have used the terms *slow-learner, educable, trainable,* and *total-care* to provide a framework of educational expectation. They ascribe to the slow-learner the educational provision of special attention in the regular classroom. It was the Kirk and Johnson thesis that the slow-learning child (those whose I.Q.'s were between 70 and perhaps 90) could be adequately taken care of by the regular educational program, if some remedial help were available. In any case, special class placement was not indicated since slow-learning children could, with some help and modification, learn academic subjects in the regular classroom.

Kirk and Johnson indicated that the trainable mentally-retarded child was capable of learning the elements of self-care, acceptable social adjustment, and economic usefulness under conditions of adequate supervision and control, such as those found in an institution, in a home or a sheltered workshop, under the guidance of understanding and accepting adults. It was toward the education of the educable mentally-

retarded youngster (those with I.Q.'s between 50 and 75 or 80)
that Kirk and Johnson pointed their educational procedures.
Based on the educational expectation of academic achievement to about the fourth grade level in school and independent or semi-independent vocational and social skills which
could be developed under an adequate training program, this
classic book presents a systematic program for the development of the academic and social skills.

Mental retardation as adaptive behavior

In 1959 the American Association on Mental Deficiency
published an inclusive definition developed by a committee
headed by Heber.[13] This definition states that mental retardation refers to sub-average intellectual functioning which origi-
nates during the developmental period and is associated with
impairment in one or more of the following: (1) maturation, *HEBER*
(2) learning, and (3) social adjustment. Later the conditions of *CLASSIFICATION*
maturation, learning, and social adjustment were replaced by
the phrase "adaptive behavior." It is clear that such a definition cuts across all of the areas: medical, social, and psychological. In addition it presents mental retardation as a generic
term (appropriate for any level of below normal mental functioning) and substitutes the levels of *mild, moderate,* and
severe as classifications to replace the older terms of *feeble-
minded* (or *moron*), *imbecile,* and *idiot.*

Curricular considerations

It should be clear that none of the definitions discussed
offer a precise enough description of either the causes or
consequences of mental retardation to provide a sufficient
basis for the development of a curriculum. Binet's definition
of a lack of memory and foresight, sequential ideas, and inability to solve puzzles, may provide good clues for techniques of teaching, but what needs to be taught is not even

hinted at. Furthermore, the medical, sociological, and educational classifications are not of great help either. A curricular system must have a philosophical base—a description of attainable goals which the training program may help the student to achieve, based on defensible assumptions of the causes and consequences of mental retardation. Jordan[14] has ably demonstrated that the use of the construct to mean different things to different people makes this impossible. As a consequence, educational efforts are notable for their diversity. However, some clue to a successful training program for the mentally subnormal can be gained by examining the significant changes in educational provisions as they have occurred through the years.

Educational history
Institutions

As early as 1818, an American asylum for the "deaf and dumb" was started in Hartford, Connecticut, but the first institution for mental defectives was not opened until 1848 at Barre, Massachusetts. The early history of institutions for the mentally retarded in the United States is actually a history of education. Howe[15] and others have indicated the purposes of the institutions as being primarily those of special training. It is quite evident, however, that a strong interest in eugenics operated in most of the institutional programs. This is supported by reports of a rather startling increase in institutional placements beginning in the early 1900's. Presumably the Kallikak study of Goddard,[16] caused many people to believe that the institutional placement of persons thought to be mentally retarded would eliminate much of the criminal element in society. Furthermore, there seemed to be a feeling that locking up the mentally retarded and segregating men and women would prevent propagation and, thus, prevent mentally retarded children from being born in the next generation. This kind of thinking was reflected in the training programs in the institutions. If the institutions had any program at all, it was to train the inmates as workers within the institutions, not to train them for independent living in a society outside of the institution. This educational work in institutions seems not far removed from the fatalistic treatment of extermination or asylum. There seemed to be no real optimistic expectation that much improvement in behavior could be expected.

At the present time all fifty states support institutions for mentally retarded individuals. They vary greatly in efficiency and programming. Some admit that they only take care of the physical needs of the retarded: they feed them, keep them warm, and protect them from dangers. Other institutions, having excellent programs in training and rehabilitation, are *VOC. REHAB.* trying to prepare the youth and older patients, if at all possible, for parole, placement, and eventual release outside the institution. The quality of the programs at state institutions has improved greatly in the last ten years. Much of this can be credited to parents' groups who became interested and helped to improve some of the less desirable institutional practices. Other states provided adequate financial support which made possible more and better buildings, and a professionally trained staff.

In modern institutions the emphasis has shifted from custodial programs to rehabilitation programs. The programs have changed from training the patients to be contented, useful, and docile in their institutional lives, to preparing them academically, personally, socially, and vocationally for lives outside the institutions. This represents a radical shift in philosophy and an unmistakable declaration of belief in the effect of environment on mental functioning.

Early curricula

Itard[17] was probably the first educator to propose a philosophical basis for an educational program—in short, a basis for a curriculum. Like John Locke, Itard believed that the mind of the newborn infant was a blank to be written on by experience. Since both Itard and Seguin aimed at the correction of mental retardation by providing rich and varied sensory experience, their sense-training curriculum was a pioneering attempt to achieve this goal.

Decroly[18] and his student, Descoudres,[19] in Belgium, refined, extended, and modified this curriculum. The infinitely practical and ingenious methods of sense training were tied to an academic curriculum. Nevertheless, it is quite clear that their educational aim was not much different from that of Itard and Sequin: namely, the cure or amelioration of mental retardation.

Inskeep[20] apparently accepted as the general aims of education for the mentally retarded, the aims of education for normal children. This program was a watered-down version of the regular academic curriculum; everything the same but modified to fit the mental level and the rate of mental development of each retarded child. The very vagueness of the general aims of education would seem to contribute little to the understanding of what should be curricular considerations for the mentally retarded. It is doubtful that much of practical value could be the consequence of such a program.

Duncan[21] in contrast to Inskeep felt the need to stress the practical arts. His curriculum was a highly realistic program in which was taught homemaking, woodworking, bee-keeping, and other tasks common to English lower-class living. Such an approach was practical, but it was also limiting. By stressing the specific skills involved in washing a dish or sweeping a floor, he allowed for no development of transfer or generalized skills of a modifable nature. It would be quite difficult to understand how anything other than frustration would be the consequence of this narrowly trained individual in interactions with a rapidly changing world.

Ingram[22] has developed a curriculum made up of units of experience which take into account the daily needs of all developing children. This seems to be the first recognition of the importance of social interaction and social skills as a vital component in the adult life of a retarded person. But the approach lacks a systematic, sequential development of the social skills. Since it is based instead on the needs of the moment, it is conceivable that for some children the necessary and particular social skills might never be learned because they are never identified as an immediate and apparent need. Nevertheless, this curriculum marks a milestone in the progress of training programs for the mentally retarded.

Kirk and Johnson[23] present a complete program for the education of retarded children. Their proposal has elements of the best suggestions of Itard, Decroly, Descoudres, Duncan, and Ingram plus approaches and activities based on the associationist's laws of learning. Such a comprehensive effort can scarcely be judged as anything but monumental; yet a clear picture of the exact end-product of the system is absent. It is not evident from the procedures just what kind of individuals will be produced if the system is carefully followed. It would, therefore, have to be classified as an eclectic approach. No great fault can be found with this approach. Nevertheless, the system itself, while quite specific at the primary and intermediate levels, is almost totally lacking in specific goals which need to be developed in order to contribute to the employability of the mentally retarded adolescent or adult.

ECLECTIC APPROACH

EXTERMINATION
REDICULE
ASYLUM
EDUCATION

Changing public school emphasis

In the public schools readily identifiable changes in practice have been evident. The first practice could be termed the "dumping grounds." This practice was one wherein all problem children were placed in one class whether their problems were ones of behavior, social maladjustment, mental retardation, or mental illness.

The second change was one which afforded "relief" for the teacher. The practice in this program was to relieve regular class teachers from all their problem pupils no matter what the pupils' problem happened to be: physical handicaps, hearing handicaps, retardation, or behavior problems. It was somewhat similar to the "dumping grounds." Contributing to both practices was the absence of valid methods for determining the causes of school failure. It was not until the various revisions of the Binet test were available (notably the 1916 revision) that a convenient method for diagnosis was available. Only then was it possible to form special classes for children with retardation, emotional problems, home difficulties, etc.

This led to the third change which may be called the "happiness" practice. Under this system the children were placed in special classes and, above all, the teacher tried to make them happy. Whether academic training took place or progress was made in the area of social adjustment was not important. What was important was that the child be happy.

Gradually, and partly because the teachers found their pupils enjoyed arts and crafts, a fourth emphasis developed. This is characterized by "crafts." Teachers were recruited from arts and crafts areas, home economics, and industrial arts. It was believed that because the child was not successful in academic work, he could work well with his hands. He was taught to make things such as shoeshine boxes, what-not shelves, hot-pad holders, or rugs. In some cases, the children were actually exploited because the finished products were sold for profit.

The assumption that the mentally subnormal are endowed with good manual dexterity has never been demonstrated; therefore such a practice is based on an unproved assumption. Furthermore, many of the arts and crafts projects were of little use and were seen primarily as busywork by the pupils. Thus, the program tended to be self-defeating.

A fifth change may be identified as "remedial-academic." Under this influence, it was felt that the only need of the child was academic success. If he could read and write, he would be successful in society. Day after day, hour after hour, the teacher would teach the academic subjects using much repetition in trying to teach these children academic skills and competencies. Not only was this repetition dreadfully dull, even when disguised in game form, but it often lacked meaning to the students. Also, it did not orient the students toward any meaningful or recognizable goals. Thus, the activity was often seen as futile; half-hearted participation was a commonly observed behavior, and many students quit school as soon as legally permitted to do so.

Several attempts have been made to spell out curricula appropriate to the mentally retarded. Many of these have been detailed in curriculum guides developed by teachers in local school systems. Generally these have had as a base the agreed upon goals of the local school system as modified to meet the needs of the educable mentally retarded pupils. As the goals and modifications seem appropriate to other school systems and special programs, so are these curriculum guides useful. Additionally, most contain methods and materials which have been developed by teachers in special classes. Their usability and practicality are, therefore, assured.

Probably the most comprehensive of the curriculum guides is that developed by teachers in the state of Illinois under the guidance and direction of Goldstein and Seigel.[24] Using a modification of the "persistent life problems" suggested by Stevens,[25] this guide suggests goals, methods, materials, and activities for the development of each of the life functions at the primary, intermediate, and advanced levels. The logic of the "life problems" and the experiences of the teachers from widely diverse geographical and cultural school areas make this a highly usable instrument. However, the lack of specific vocational objectives at the high school level tends to limit it. Furthermore, "persistent life problems" were decided on by the authors through rational or logical thought rather than as a consequence of empirical or research analysis. Thus, these "persistent life problems" are *thought* to be important to the education of the mentally subnormal pupil, but they have not been *proved* to be important.

Educational practice and theory

Each of these practices has extended improvements and modifications of programs developed by prior educators. In application they far outstrip concommitant educational theory. That is, each change has generally been an improvement from the preceding practice which has come about because of fortuitous circumstances. Homogeneous classes for the mentally retarded, free of children with emotional or other educational problems, for example, could not be started until the Binet test became generally available. The fact that practices have changed is a tribute to the dedication of teachers in the field who have applied their best thinking to improving the teaching for their students. But fundamental educational thought seems not to have affected practice materially. Ideally, educational philosophy should provide the basis from which curricular patterns can be developed deductively. The vagueness of the concept "mental retardation" may be at fault. That it does not refer to precisely stated premises and assumptions concerning the cause, nature, and characteristics, may be a reason for the lack of axiological statements from which appropriate educational practice can receive impetus and direction. Both Itard and Sequin, for example, believed mental retardation to be caused by lack of stimuli reaching the brain. The blank mind written on by experience was the axiom upon which they based their educational efforts. From this position, educational practice was, logically, to present sensory stimuli of a variety and intensity thought necessary to produce a civilized human being.

Such a deductive approach to a systematic educational program is only as good as the axiom from which it is deduced. Theory, as it relates to mental retardation now rejects the "tabula rasa" description of the mind of a newborn infant.

Unfortunately no similarly incompassing axiom has been suggested to replace the discarded Locke formulation.

In the absence of such an axiological foundation for educational practices, there is the alternative of finding some defensible empirical base. Although interference with the ability to learn is a universally observed characteristic of the mentally subnormal this is not a sufficient base upon which to build an educational program. *Learning* in this context is not clearly understood. The unanswered questions of what kind of *learning*, verbal, academic, motor, social or personal, continue to plague curriculum planners. Investigations such as those by House and Zeaman,[26] Cantor and Hottel[27] and Stolurow[28] have demonstrated learning curves from mentally-subnormal persons not different in form from those of laboratory animals or college Sophomores in specific, isolated, learning tasks. This seems to argue against a universally acceptable theory of learning specific to the mental subnormal at this time. Instead, it pinpoints the necessity of searching in a different direction for guides to use in developing a sound educational program.

In 1959 the committee on nomenclature of the American Association on Mental Deficiency report refers to subaverage intellectual functioning associated with impairment of maturation, learning, and social adjustment or adaptive behavior. The key phrase "subaverage intellectual functioning" focuses attention on intelligence test performance. Thus mental retardation in a generic sense is defined by a statistical judgment of the intelligence quotient earned by an individual on an intelligence test like the Binet.

The circularity of that statement becomes even more apparent when the items which make up the test are then used as the delineation of the characteristics of the mentally retarded. Yet the one characteristic held in common by this group is "subaverage" intelligence test performance. In the absence of evidence that this sub-average performance is caused by sensory or emotional factors, one can only conclude that it is the result of some kind of inferior intellect. Thus mental subnormality is defined as subaverage intelligence test performance.

There is abundant evidence that it is reasonable to expect improvement in behavior in the mentally retarded as a result of training. The problem then becomes one of finding goals for training which are feasible. Of the changes in educational practice mentioned, most are based on a teacher's judgment of what skills the mentally retarded should be taught. None of the changes in educational practice has as a basis findings from investigations of factors which characterize those mentally retarded persons who are making a successful adjustment to society or those who are not. The programs suffer from a lack of research evidence into what factors or characteristics contribute to successful adult living and occupational adequacy. If a program is designed to produce an occupationally adequate and socially independent adult, it should be based on a consideration of the characteristics and needs of the individual being served, and should make systematic provisions for the development of those skills which have been found to be necessary for independent living and occupational adequacy. Just what these characteristics for successful adjustment are is not clear from the definitions or educational programs reviewed.

It is necessary to turn to the published research and program descriptions to find guidelines for the development of a reasonable secondary work-study program for mentally subnormal young people. Such an approach to program development lacks validity in a deductive sense but is strengthened because it contains elements which are based on the best of past and current practices.

The program presented in this book presumes that despite individual variability, the mentally subnormal person will have poor memory, inferior ability to profit from instruction, limited ability to generalize, difficulty in noting relationships, unreliable judgment, and little foresight, as demonstrated by subaverage intelligence test performance. The program further presumes that these characteristics can be improved through a carefully planned sequence of educational experiences. It rests squarely on the belief that the level of mental functioning is affected by environmental influences and can be improved by education. Furthermore, the kinds of educational procedures determine the direction of the development. Therefore the educational program should be developed from what can be learned about those mentally subnormal persons who are making a successful adjustment to the world of work.

Thus the program is based on the demands of the present complex society and the modern political philosophy which stresses the need for each individual to understand what is required of a citizen in a democratic society and to be responsible for his own behavior and economic productivity.[29]

2

CHARACTERISTICS AND CURRICULAR NEEDS

OF THE MENTALLY SUBNORMAL

OUR public schools have more pupils than ever before who are, if they are to become occupationally adequate, in need of special help. The reasons for this situation are many.

First, in most states there has been an increase in the number of programs for mentally handicapped children at the elementary level. These special programs have kept many students enrolled in school who might have dropped out had they attended regular classes. Second, more mentally retarded go on to high school because of the many special programs in the elementary schools and because of compulsory school attendance laws. Pupils can no longer quit school because they are academically unsuccessful. Third, unions, fair trade employment practices, and state and federal laws make it difficult for a sixteen-year-old child to obtain employment. Also, there are fewer jobs available for a sixteen-year-old boy. For example, the Western Union telegraph boy, the traveler on the bicycle, has been replaced by the telephone or the intercom system. All these combine to swell the high school rolls with students who have little aptitude for or interest in academic programs.

High schools have been forced to try to accommodate mentally subnormal pupils in some manner. Many have relied on placement in regular classes. In this arrangement no academic adjustment is made and the students are placed in regular classes with their normal, bright, and gifted peers. They take the traditional curriculum of mathematics, English, Latin, history, and social studies. Failure and dropout are regular concommitants because of the unattainable standards of achievement required.

Some schools have a three-track system. In the three-track system, the same curriculum is offered and the same educational objectives are pursued. One track is for the bright student, another for the average student, and the third is for the slow learners and the retarded. The program for the slow group may be offered at a reduced rate and the content is generally watered-down, but it does not meet the educational needs of this last group. It is an academic curriculum offered at a slow pace.

If a remedial program is provided, classes of remedial reading, remedial English, and remedial arithmetic are offered—sometimes for no credit. The student is upgraded, when he has been successful in his remedial courses, and he takes his place in the regular program. This is a traditional curriculum that is offered to these children. Although it recognizes the limited abilities of the students and tries to do something about them, it still is academic and inappropriate.

Vocational programs have been established in a number of schools which have found that slow learners have not been successful in the traditional academic classes. They have placed these children in shop, home economics, physical education, chorus, and in some other music courses. This, too, has not worked out very well because the slow learner and retarded many times cannot read the material used. For example, in home economics the girls may not be able to modify a recipe or may not be able to measure amounts expressed in fractions. The boys may have difficulty in measuring, or understanding dimensions involving fractions. High school music classes have been a disappointment because many of them require a student to be able to read music.

Many of these students cannot read the printed words, and reading music is an even more difficult task. In physical education classes many of them have difficulty because of poor co-ordination, inability to follow directions, or inability to remember some of the intricate instructions or plays that are necessary in highly organized games.

The academically oriented, special class high school program specifically for the educable mentally handicapped differs from the regular class program in that only certified educable mentally handicapped students are eligible and the teacher must be a person trained according to the standards set up usually by a state department of public instruction or comparable body. It is traditional in that it includes all the academic courses found in regular high school programs, such as general science, general mathematics, general English, and sometimes even a language. The classes are usually a bit smaller than the regular classes, and in some cases an individual program is planned for each child. The students may be sent out of their special room to take physical education, shop, or music with their regular high school peers, but they return to the special class for academic work. The goals are still academic. Generally no attempt to include specific vocational training is evident.

That these provisions are inappropriate is attested to by Binzberg,[1] Ribicoff,[2] Havighurst and Stiles,[3] Bowman and Matthews,[4] and Conant,[5] and many other observers. Requirements for successful participation are generally beyond the mental level of these mentally subnormal youngsters. Even when the academic offerings are "adjusted" to the students' mental levels, the contents of the program do not seem to lead to a goal that can be perceived as important by the students. These youngsters often feel that school attendance means "putting in time" which will do them little good toward getting jobs.

An additional criticism may be justly leveled at the procedural adjustments. The steps are not systematically programmed and the students' participation and progress are not readily apparent—there is no easily understood feedback of information about the students' progress.

It appears that a different kind of school curriculum is necessary to prepare these youth for a satisfactory role in society as adults in the world of work. The learning experiences that they have must be meaningful to enable them to have the experiences which will point to later success. Additionally, the experiences should promote adequate personal and social adjustment in the acquisition of knowledges, skills, habits, and attitudes that they will need to become successful employees. What these experiences should be is determined by the characteristics of the youngsters and an examination of the kinds of behaviors required to live successfully in the world of work.

Characteristics

The term mentally subnormal, used as a generic term, includes both the group with I.Q.'s from 75 to 90 (often called the "slow learners") and the educable mentally retarded group (I.Q.'s ranging from about 50 to 75). Statistically, about 16 per cent of the population would test in this broad I.Q. range. Their achievement test scores indicate mastery of educational fundamentals at about the second-, third-, fourth-, or fifth-grade level. Quite often, although they are able to read at one of these lower levels, because they are in high school they will be assigned to read a high school book at a tenth-, eleventh-, or twelfth-grade level: an impossible assignment.

Physically this group will look very much like their normal and gifted peers. Some of them will be very mature individuals, others will be small for their age, but generally they will differ in physical co-ordination and in size as much as their normal peers differ. Socially they have the same needs as their normal peers and will show a normal interest in members of the opposite sex. They will be interested in talking to them or going to a dance just as other high school students, but the mentally subnormal may not be as successful in these activities as the rest of their schoolmates. They may not have the social graces and know-how to behave in a manner acceptable to members of the opposite sex.

If they have not had the advantage of placement in a class for the educable mentally handicapped in their elementary school years, some of them will have developed some attitudes and habits towards school that are not desirable. If it has been the policy of the school to promote slow learners "socially," their academic achievement level may be several years lower than the level to which they have been promoted. Some may have developed a number of undesirable personality traits because of the learning difficulties they have encountered. Recognition of some kind seems to be a need of all individuals, and not having received recognition from their peers or teachers for academic competencies, they may try to gain it through other less socially acceptable attention-getting devices.

In addition to retarded mental development, some students in this group may come from an economically impoverished background. They may have had few academic advantages in the home and little interest or desire to learn anything of a "book" nature. For them it will be necessary to develop socially accepted attitudes and a desire to want to learn things that will help them to become successful citizens in our society.

Others will have had learning problems due to something other than a poor cultural background. Many times this group is referred to as the "brain-injured" group. This may be a confusing label. Perhaps they should be regarded simply as a group with learning problems rather than a brain-injured group. They frequently come from a very good social-economic background, but for some reason they experience severe difficulty in learning. They have a desire to learn; they come from a background where learning is the thing to do; and their intelligence test results seem to point out that they have adequate intelligence to learn certain things; nevertheless they have been unable to learn. Some will have accompanying visual, hearing, coordination problems or aphasic conditions which may necessitate certain special adjustments in their school programs. This group needs special remedial techniques that are appropriate to their learning difficulties.

In most cities in the United States the high school program is geared to the average and above average individual. Thus, the mentally subnormal group find it difficult to meet the standards imposed upon them by this curriculum. Not only do they find difficulty in meeting the academic standards, but they also find it extremely difficult to adjust to the behavior standards set up by the conventional high school. Lack of successful experiences in the high schools encourages them to drop out of school. Often when they try to enter the work-a-day world they meet the new and additional frustration of being unable to find employment. They seek employment with few or no skills to offer an employer and also with questionable ability to meet adult behavior standards. They lack skills the employer may be looking for and the essential attitudes and habits towards work which make prognosis for employment favorable.

The usual history of the education of the mentally subnormal child is not a pleasant one, and as a result, his attitude toward school and toward teachers is generally not one of understanding. He was probably forced into reading before his mental age was high enough for him to comprehend reading, or he entered into the reading situation with (if he came from a culturally deprived environment) a very limited background of understanding. If such is the case, it is a common practice in many elementary schools to fail or hold back the mentally subnormal child for one or two years. In most states compulsory education laws have forced the mentally subnormal child to remain in school until he is sixteen years of age. His history during that time would typically involve several retentions and eventually some social promotion whether or not he had comprehended or mastered the academics presented at each grade level. He is usually overage and oversize for the grade he is in. This further tends to complicate his feelings of inadequacy or inferiority and generally leaves the street wide open for antisocial behavior or something referred to as delinquent or pre-delinquent behavior.

Children having I.Q.'s of between 50 and 80 or 90 are usually unable to master the traditional high school curriculum. All of these students need to be taught the kinds of skills which they will need to maintain themselves. They need a curriculum which is based on a determination of the skills needed for independent living and occupational adequacy. To complicate the problem, a large number of school dropouts, delinquents, and unemployed youth are found in this group. Many youngsters of the school-age population from grades seven through twelve drop out of school before they receive a high school diploma. These dropouts usually encounter great difficulty in finding a job and in continuing to hold it. In addition to limited mental ability, many school dropouts, delinquents, and unemployed youth come from culturally deprived homes which have contributed to questionable moral values and social behavior and make it even more difficult for them to find and continue employment.

The mentally subnormal group is rapidly becoming the most important school and community problem. Studies on juvenile delinquency, dropouts, and unemployment consistently report that the mean intelligence quotient of this group falls somewhere between 80 and 90. "According to recent investigations, about one out of every three dropouts from school systems leaves during the eighth grade or before; two out of three never get to senior high school, i.e., they drop out before the tenth grade."[6]

This publication further states that to effect a solution,

first is the necessity—since a large proportion of the drop-outs are retarded in the early grades and actually leave school well before the completion of high school—to consider the development of programs of guidance and counseling at the elementary school level. The second relates to the possibility of increasing the "holding power" of the school through the design of courses in instruction which can hold interest of and be of substantive value to some of the young people who did not make any progress within the existing curriculum.

School officials are faced with an ever increasing number of young people who have a restricted potential for learning, limited academic skills, may exhibit unacceptable personal and social behavior, have little desire for or need of an academic educational program, are limited in their vocational experiences and desires, and are in imminent danger of becoming school failures, dropouts, and, perhaps, delinquents.

There has been a history of educational provisions for the mentally handicapped which is essentially categorical in nature. The mentally subnormal have been divided by intelligence quotients into rather discreet groups, such as slow learners (I.Q.'s 75 or so to about 90), educable mentally handicapped (I.Q.'s roughly between 50 and about 75), trainable mentally handicapped (I.Q.'s from about 25 or so to about 50), and custodial (I.Q.'s generally below about 25). Research shows clearly that this system of classification is useless in vocational training (*see* pp. 43–44). It therefore seems impossible to categorize children neatly by I.Q.'s into groups that will or will not profit from a vocational or work-study program without great possibility of misjudgment. Accordingly, the arbitrary divisions of slow learner, educable, and trainable are not used in this program. Instead, the term *mentally subnormal* is used so that great latitude is allowed for entry into the program and individual progress will be the criteria used to determine continuing eligibility.

Empirical considerations for curriculum

The word *curriculum*, as applied to education, has come to mean "a course of study or a series of courses which are aimed at a particular goal." One of the primary goals of the education for mentally subnormal adolescents is that of occupational adequacy and includes all of the related skills which are included in that goal. In the absence of an axiological basis for establishing curriculum, the outlining of a course of study must come from a study of what characteristics are possessed by subnormal individuals who have been found to be occupationally adequate.

Many investigators have conducted follow-up studies of adult mentally retarded individuals. Studies, such as those by Baller[7] and Charles[8] in 1936 and in 1953 respectively, and the work of Kennedy[9] in 1948, and Phelps[10] in 1956, provide conclusive evidence of the fact that a substantial majority of the mentally subnormal do become occupationally and socially adequate during their adult years. Studies by Channing[11] in 1932 and Keys and Nathan[12] in 1932 demonstrate that the mentally subnormal are successful in clerical work, service occupations, some aspects of agriculture, manufacturing, transportation, the trades industries, public service, and personal service. They also offer evidence that these individuals with some rare exceptions confine their activities to the unskilled or semiskilled work categories.

Attempts to identify the characteristics which make for success in the various levels of work have not been particularly successful. Studies by Fryer,[13] and Raymond[14] during the 1920's on minimum intelligence levels required in specific occupations found that with minimum intellectual skills, the performance of individuals was not directly related to intelligence. This finding has been substantiated by many recent investigators and the conclusion is that intelligence, by itself, is not a good basis for predicting vocational efficiency for the mentally subnormal.

Rautman[15] in 1949 suggested that a better prognosis exists for the subnormal from poor homes than from good homes. However, this was not substantiated by Shafter[16] in 1957. Other investigators, notably Cowan and Goldman[17] in 1959, and Neff[18] in 1959, have pointed to the need for information on the degree of family support which the individual may get as an important factor in his employability.

Efforts to study the effect of age on employability have been complicated by the fact that so many of the investigators have studied only people within a restricted age range and thus real differences could not be determined. Efforts to determine the effect of sibling rank in the family have met with little success. Likewise, the studies have been controversial in establishing the degree to which physical appearance and physical condition have an effect on the employability of the mentally subnormal. By the same token, investigations on the effect of the number of years in school, the academic achievement, and the number of years spent in special classes have not been fruitful. More recent attempts to get at the factors of personality and work habits have been slightly more helpful. Although the trend seems to be to attempt to be objective in studies in personality characteristics and work habit characteristics by the use of rating scales or checklists, the results are still equivocal.[19]

It seems highly probable that the employability of the mentally subnormal is dependent upon a number of different factors working in concert or compensating for each other. Such things as intelligence, academic skills, personal factors, social factors, environmental or support factors, and vocational skills are no doubt interrelated. A realistic curriculum for secondary school programs for the mentally subnormal must take them into account.

A grant from the Office of Vocational Rehabilitation was obtained in 1957 for the establishment of an Employment Evaluation and Training Project at Southern Illinois University.[20] This started as an eighteen-week program. Mentally subnormal males over sixteen years of age who were clients of the State of Illinois Division of Vocational Rehabilitation from various parts of the state were referred to the Southern Illinois University project for service. On acceptance, these trainees were taken into the project in groups of four. The first three weeks of their stay were devoted to Vocational Evaluation and Testing: an intensive evaluation of their skills and abilities on tasks of a light industrial, business and clerical, and service nature, as well as information from formal tests and attitude scales. Special attention was paid to the personal-social behavior of each trainee in his relations with his supervisors and his peers.

At the end of three weeks a decision was made as to whether each client would be able to profit from the next fifteen-week part of the program: Vocational Adjustment Training. In this part of the program, the clients were placed on jobs for three-week periods. In all, they had experience in five different jobs during their fifteen weeks of Vocational Adjustment Training.

Upon completion, the clients were returned to their home communities where the local rehabilitation counselor used the information from the reports of the Employment Evaluation and Training Project to help him search for employment possibilities for the client. To help the counselor in this task, an intake and follow-up supervisor was available for consultation.

During the three-week evaluation phase of the program, each trainee was evaluated on twenty-eight specific tasks. These tasks were designed to measure certain skills important to employment in service occupations, light industrial work, and business and clerical work. The characteristics observed in the evaluation phase are:

1] dexterity, coordination, discrimination, and mobility
2] attention span, cooperation, willingness, and initiative
3] amount of supervision and directions needed to perform the task
4] ability to count, alphabetize, and make change
5] reaction to criticism, supervision, and evaluations
6] ability to work independently and with others
7] self-confidence and sense of responsibility
8] sociability as indicated by verbal exchange, manners, consideration for others, and social sensitivity
9] ability to follow a routine or to stick with a task
10] judgment or confidence in a work situation or the ability to make decisions
11] responsibility for making an adequate personal appearance

The trainee was rated on each of these characteristics by the evaluators. The ratings were summarized in order to present a profile picture of the abilities (and disabilities) of the client. In addition to the evaluation, during this phase of the program each trainee received a medical examination; a speech and hearing examination; and was tested using the Wechsler Adult Intelligence Scale, part of the Differential Aptitude Test, the appropriate forms of the California Test of Achievement in reading and arithmetic, and part of the Minnesota Clerical Test. The results of his performance on these tests became a part of his permanent record and were used in the analysis of the differences between clients who became employed and those who did not after the program was finished.

The fifteen-week Vocational Adjustment Training phase of the program provided trainees with three-week experience on each of five different jobs. While the Vocational Evaluation and Testing phase of the program was specifically designed to determine what intellectual and vocational skills the trainee might have, the Vocational Adjustment phase of the program was designed, to evaluate the trainee's use of his vocational and intellectual skills in a real job situation and to give him experience in different areas of work with which he may have been unfamiliar. The jobs which were selected for use are the following types:

1] FOOD SERVICE—such as cafeteria and small individual drive-in variety

The work includes such things as washing dishes, cleaning the kitchen area, food preparation, taking orders, serving customers, both machine and manual dishwashing, and the preparation of such things as hamburgers, coffee, salads, vegetables, meats, and bakery goods.

2] GENERAL SERVICE WORK—such as greenhouse, supermarket, and automobile service station work

This includes such things as cutting, potting, watering, and generally caring for plants, planting flowers, mixing soils, and even making decorations; stocking shelves with merchandise, pricing, changing prices, cutting and packaging produce, and carrying out groceries; pumping gas, checking oil, washing cars, changing tires, cleaning windshields, and generally waiting on customers.

3] JANITORIAL SERVICE—both in hospitals and in living quarters

This includes such things as sweeping, dusting, mopping, preparing and carrying ice to rooms, tending the furnace, caring for grounds, handyman duties, washing laundry, and setting tables.

4] JOBS OF LIGHT INDUSTRIAL NATURE

This includes such things as printshop work, athletic equipment repair, drycleaning and warehouse work, and such specialized tasks as working on both simple and complex machines for collating and assembly work; general delivery service; cutting, cleaning, and otherwise preparing books for rebinding; cleaning, refinishing, and binding the books themselves as well as map repair and map preservation; included also would be industrial work either of tearing down equipment or repairing various kinds of equipment. In warehouse work such things as loading and unloading trucks, storing fruit and other materials and sorting and collecting were done. To some degree clerical tasks were made available either through the University Textbook Service and the Registrar's Office where simple filing and recording of student records were practiced.

All in all, the experience was designed to provide as many different types of experiences as possible to the trainees in order to find out in which area they may show the greatest aptitude for employability.

For each job a checklist was filled out by the employer. These were used in an accumulated form to indicate a general total and average rating of the employee by the employer. The form used was a modification of one designed by Warren.[21] It is made up of lists of specific characteristics of behavior arranged in two groups. The first group is a list of personality and social adjustment characteristics. It lists such items as self-confidence, cheerfulness, and cooperation. The second group is concerned with the work habits and efficiency of the trainees and contains such items as promptness, safety consciousness, care with materials and property, and quality of work. The third group of questions are general. They involve overall questions on efficiency and personal and social conduct on which a rating is given by the employer.

One of the unique characteristics of this checklist is a question in which the employer is asked to indicate whether he would be willing to hire this individual if a job were available. This question made it possible to find out whether the employer felt that the most important limiting aspect of the trainee's behavior was his personality or his work efficiency and the relative amount which each might play in the decision to hire the individual. Furthermore, it provided a built-in system of checks and balances so that the staff supervisor could get a precise statement from the employer concerning the factors which limit the employability of the trainee.

All ratings were made on the basis of whether an individual was average, above average, or below average. Several other scoring arrangements were tried, but it became apparent that the one which was most meaningful to the employers was that which used as its basis the general concept of average performance. Although this was not as precise as some may wish it to be, it had the advantage of being readily understood by the employers. Since a composite or an average rating from five different employers was used to arrive at a score for each of the trainees, this was found to be a valid method for determining the trainee's potential for employment.

During their time in the project, all of the trainees were housed in a dormitory supervised by houseparents. The dormitory contained two areas for sleeping. Each area housed a maximum of ten to twelve trainees. On the first floor was the lounge separated from both the dormitory and the eating area, and arranged so that it afforded a considerable amount of privacy. A television set and a radio-phonograph were available with chairs for lounging and desks and tables for writing letters.

The houseparents occupied a private apartment separated from the dormitory and eating area. The apartment had its own private entrance, but it also had another entrance which allowed close supervision of the dormitory and eating areas without actually being in them. Bath and toilet facilities for the trainees were provided in close proximity to the sleeping area. In addition, an office and a room for supervisors' helpers were close to the sleeping and lounging areas.

The program provided for all hours of the day, including

those of evaluation, of work, and for evenings and weekends. Activities were designed to provide training in the following:

1] establish regular living habits (rising and retiring at reasonable times and getting enough sleep)
2] personal grooming
3] care of personal effects (clothing, etc.)
4] care of property (not lying down on the couch with shoes on, etc.)
5] discretion in the use of money
6] learning how to do things of a recreational nature (playing baseball, bowling, participating in spectator activities)
7] developing adequate table manners
8] practice recognizing, evaluating and attempting to solve personal problems
9] evaluation of jobs in terms of vacations, fringe benefits, job requirements, and job satisfaction
10] help in recognizing personal abilities and limitations and their implications

Opportunity to observe the trainee's success in the above was provided.

Personnel for the residence area in addition to the houseparents consisted of a cook and two part-time supervisors. Medical services were available as well as special testing services. For each trainee a $4-a-week allowance was provided from which he had to pay for all his recreation, cigarettes, shaving equipment, and other personal needs.

Prior to the trainee's returning to his home, an interview was held by the intake and follow-up supervisor. During the interview, a definite arrangement was made for a time when the supervisor would visit the trainee in his local community to attempt a job placement. Prior to the trainee's leaving, the intake and follow-up supervisor had access to the records of progress of each trainee; had discussed him in the weekly staff meeting; and had the recommendations of the vocational evaluation and testing supervisor, the vocational adjustment training supervisor, and the houseparents to guide him in searching for a job for the trainee.

In the local community the supervisor sometimes accompanied the local counselor in the search for possible work placement for the trainee. In other instances, the supervisor may have had to use the want ads of the local newspaper to get his leads for possible jobs. In still other instances, he simply made a "cold" approach on a door-to-door basis looking for the types of jobs suitable for this particular client. Occasionally, contacts were made through the local employment service.

Once a contact with a potential employer was made, the approach emphasized that the prospective employee was not a neophyte but an adult who had worked for five previous employers. In this contact the supervisor had with him the forms, evaluations, and reports of the previous employers and went over these, sometimes in great detail, with the prospective employer. Generally, all of the conversation was very positive in nature: describing the assets of the trainee and in a sense giving the trainee an ideal to live up to.

Follow-up after a placement was of an informal nature and was conducted when the intake and follow-up supervisor happened to be in that immediate vicinity. However, each trainee had the services of his local rehabilitation counselor to whom he could turn for both counseling and guidance.

In order to examine differences between employed and unemployed trainees eighty-two former trainees from the Employment Evaluation and Training Project were studied.[22] Information on background, intelligence, academic achievement, performance on evaluation tasks and ratings by employers on personality and work efficiency factors was collected, and subjected to statistical analysis. Some ninety-one specific variables were examined.

Only mentally subnormal males above the age of sixteen were accepted as trainees in the Employment Evaluation and

Training Project. Due to changes in the program, eighty-two former trainees who had had approximately equivalent experiences in the program and on whom approximately the same information was available for analysis were selected for comparison. They divided by chance into two equal groups. Forty-one succeeded in securing employment after leaving the project and are referred to as the "employed group," while forty-one failed to secure employment and are referred to as the "unemployed group." Ages ranged from sixteen to forty with a median of nineteen, and WAIS Full Scale I.Q.'s fell between 50 and 95 with a median of 76. In common, all were referred by the Illinois State Division of Vocational Rehabilitation because .they were considered unemployable by the counselor in their local communities. They came from small, medium, and large cities, from state institutions, and from a variety of home backgrounds.

No differences in intelligence were found between the employed group and the unemployed group. This was determined from scores made on the Wechsler Adult Intelligence Scale. The clients were first analyzed in terms of their full-scale scores; then differences were sought between the performance scores of the two groups; and finally, the differences between the verbal scores of the two groups were investigated. In no instance was a difference found between the intellectual ability of those trainees who became employed after leaving the project and those who did not.

For a more detailed examination of the data, an analysis was made of the sub-test scores of the Wechsler and a difference was found only in the area of "object assembly."[23] Next, a levels analysis using the Full Scale I.Q. divisions 60–69, 70–79, and 80–89 was carried out with the expectation that perhaps those individuals who had higher intelligence test scores may have a better potential for employability. Once again no differences were found between the groups at any of these levels. Furthermore, the three trainees who had scores in the 50's became employed after leaving the project, and one client who was not in the sample but who scored in the 40's secured employment.

The implication of these findings is that the sole use of the I.Q. to determine eligibility for a class for educable mentally handicapped has to be considered questionable. However, for a large percentage the I.Q. was a good guide when other factors were also considered. In addition to I.Q., school records provide a cumulative record for many years of school experience. These can be of great aid. However, there seems to be no logical reason to exclude children who test in the 40's nor in the 80's or 90's, if I.Q. scores are the only criteria used to predict future employability for these groups. It is quite possible that an intelligence test score which is low can be compensated for by other factors which contribute to employability. In any case, it is important to avoid setting rigid limits on the range of I.Q. for youngsters to be considered for an employment program.

There was no significant difference found in the academic achievement test scores of the groups who became employed and those who did not. What difference was found indicated a very slight superiority for those individuals who did not secure employment. Furthermore, after investigating the amount of time in special classes, it became evident that there was no superiority in academic achievement among those who had spent a greater amount of time in school or a greater amount of time in a special class.

Apparently the ability to read and to write is not a critical factor in the kind of employment which those trainees secured. This does not deny that inability to read, write, make change, or do simple arithmetical computations would be a limiting factor in employability. Probably an individual who does possess these skills may be competent to be hired on a job at a somewhat higher level than one who does not possess the skills. However, the possession of the skills in and of themselves is not critical in simply getting a job. Other personal and social factors appear to be equally important and should be taken into account. If there is a choice of how time is to be spent in the classroom, it is quite probable that the academic program can be slighted but not the development of the personal, social, and vocational skills, so important in employability.

The employed and unemployed were compared on many different characteristics. One of the findings was that in regard to age virtually all of the trainees within both groups were employable. The preferred ages for employment were those between nineteen and thirty. Few of those under nineteen or over thirty were successful in seeking employment.

Because of the workman's compensation laws, businessmen are reluctant to hire anyone under eighteen. This reluctance is reinforced when the youngsters show immature behavior. It becomes doubly important that the mentally subnormal be retained in a protected environment until they became at least eighteen, if mature, and twenty-one if they are not. Therefore, it becomes the responsibility of the school program to take mentally subnormal students at the age of fourteen or fifteen and provide a program for extending them over five or six years. This would insure that they will have reached a level of maturity appropriate to the job market.

Problems having to do with vision, hearing, and orthopedic handicaps of the two groups were compared. Evidence indicated that the presence of an ancillary handicap did not prevent employment. Height and weight seem to have no influence on employability; however the employed group had a better height-weight ratio than the unemployed group, and had a better general health score as indicated by a physical examination. They seemed to be physically more adept than the unemployed group, and physically they were somewhat more attractive.

It seems apparent from the data that the *presence* of a physical handicap is less important than the *appearance* of a physical handicap. This is not an unexpected finding since people tend to shy away from those who look different. The

EMPLOYED WERE BETTER SOCIALLY DEVELOPED, HEAVIER AND TALLER THAN, NON-EMPLOYED, ALSO HAD FEWER POOR APPEARING PHYS. DISABILITIES.

implication is that it is important for the mentally subnormal group to do everything possible to avoid an unusual appearance. This suggests that a physical restoration program of both a corrective and cosmetic nature be instituted early in the school program for each individual. A special and intensive speech correction program should be available to these individuals who need it, and it would also seem to be important that a program specifically designed to provide for weight control, physical fitness training, grooming and cleanliness should be integral parts of the school program and should be started early in the career of each student. There seems little doubt that none of these personal characteristics alone are devastating to his chances for employment. For example, it is probably not detrimental for an individual to have a speech defect if he has abilities to compensate for this particular defect. However, in the total constellation of the individual's characteristics, it is quite possible that the presence of a speech defect may be one of the characteristics which would limit the probability of his employment. It follows that attention to all of the factors contributing to physical appearance of the individual is an important part of the school program.

A rating scale developed by Warren[24] and modified for this project, was filled out by each employer on each trainee for each job. Thus, average ratings on personal and social factors and on work habits were obtained for each trainee on as many as five different jobs. An analysis of the differences between the employed and the unemployed groups showed a definite superiority for the employed group in such personal and social characteristics as self-confidence, cooperation, cheerfulness, ability to accept criticism, ability to mix socially with other employees, ability to concentrate on assigned tasks, and respect for superiors. In work-efficiency characteristics only the presence of greater initiative and promptness discriminated between those who became employed and those who did not. However, in the overall ratings by the employers in the general areas of personality and work-efficiency, the employed group was clearly rated superior to the unemployed.

These behavior patterns of personality and work-efficiency are presumably the result of attitudes which are learned over a long period of time. The extent and quality of experience, the kind of reinforcement history, and the reaction held by individuals to their performance determined these very relevant behaviors. It is for this reason that early placement of the mentally subnormal in special classes should be accomplished before failure patterns and the subsequent compensations for these failure patterns are well established. It also points up the need for cooperative units of work in both the primary and intermediate elementary classes and art and crafts activities for individual accomplishments.

From the findings of the Employment Evaluation and Training Project and data from other training programs,[25] it seems clear that the high school curriculum should have the following components:

1] a curriculum which uses academic subjects, experience, work, and work evaluation to teach vocational, personal, and social skills

2] a program which extends over five or six years thus keeping the mentally subnormal students in school until they are approximately nineteen or twenty years of age

3] a program which provides for the amelioration of ancillary handicapping conditions such as poor speech, visual problems, orthopedic handicaps, and hearing problems

4] a concerted program of physical restoration including physical fitness training, cleanliness training, and grooming

5] a program which emphasizes the skills needed for independent living

6] specific curricular provisions to encourage
    A] self-confidence,

B] cooperation,

C] cheerfulness,

D] ability to accept criticism,

E] ability to mix socially,

F] ability to mind his own business,

G] initiative, and

H] respect for supervision

7] on-the-job training in high school buildings or a sheltered workshop for at least two to four hours per day during the first year

8] on-the-job training off the high school campus which should eventually involve an eight-hour, off-campus, supervised work day during the second, third, and fourth years of the program

Kirk[26] and some other authorities state that a work-experience program should be part of a post-school program. If it were a post-school program, this portion of the child's training would become the responsibility of persons other than the public school staff. Other than the public high school faculties, who is this to be? Some point to state offices of vocational rehabilitation. If it were just a matter of short-term job training, this might be the place for the program, but it is not a six-month or a one-year program. This should be the final phase of a carefully planned twelve-year curriculum for slow learners and mentally subnormal adolescents. It is not just job training, but job training plus many other aspects involved in effective living. It is a problem of coordinating social aspects, interpersonal relations, and academic subjects with a job. It is adjustment to individuals and to groups. Regular visits by a supervising counselor to assist the student to make decisions and satisfactorily to fulfill the demands of effective living and of work are imperative.

An employable individual must have a level of intellectual, personal, social and vocational skills so integrated as to make it possible for him to get and hold a job. From current information it does not seem possible to describe exactly which characteristics are most important, nor which characteristics in strength will compensate for deficiencies in other characteristics. Until such delineations are possible, the educational program should provide experiences which offer the best possibility for the fullest development of each of the characteristics identified as important to employability. These experiences should be modified or abandoned as new information becomes available.

It is here suggested that these characteristics should be the core of a curriculum for the mentally subnormal in the public schools. Specific provisions should be made in this curriculum for the development of the skills identified as being pertinent in developing the characteristics leading to effective living for the mentally subnormal. How this may be done will be described in the following chapters.

3

ORGANIZATION OF A
HIGH SCHOOL WORK-STUDY PROGRAM
FOR THE MENTALLY SUBNORMAL

Theoretical considerations

IN the absence of a defensible axiomatic base, provisions for a high school work-study program can be determined from the historical perspective or the inappropriateness of what has been provided, and the determination from research of the characteristics which need to be trained. The program still would be incomplete without an indication of the particular learning differences of this group which make it mandatory that this program be different from the offerings of a typical high school. In short, what is needed is a determination of the differences between the learning characteristics of this group and those of normal youngsters.

By definition, the mentally subnormal have a reduced capacity for learning. Numerous investigations have established that the learning level to be expected from this group will be approximately one-half to three-fourths that of normal. Probably the best single criteria of expectation is the Mental Age.[1] Unfortunately the usefulness of the Mental Age as an index of the level of expectation of learning is seriously distorted by the experiences of the students, their home backgrounds, their anxiety for academic achievement, and their sensory efficiency. Furthermore, the primary accomplishment expected from a work-study program is vocational, not academic, and virtually no clear research evidence exists which has examined the relationship between Mental Age and vocational accomplishment.

Attempts to determine whether a qualitative learning difference exists between the mentally subnormal and normal youngsters have been few and not very productive. Reviews by Dunn and Capobianco[2] and by McPherson[3] make special note of this scarcity. Only one study has authoritatively reported such a qualitative difference: that of Stedman.[4] His finding that a difference exists in the storage and retrieval functions, while of great theoretical moment, is so isolated a discovery that it does not provide much of a base for a program. Even the reports of low frustration tolerance, limited attention span and poor ability to generalize or transfer are inadequately substantiated.[5] Resting, then, on the sparce and incomplete foundations of the axiological and empirical bases, the content and directions of a training program must look for support from theoretical positions. This may be considered from two directions: counseling theory or reinforcement learning theory.

The many theoretical positions of counseling theorists have in common the changing of attitudes, behaviors and values through some kind of interpersonal interaction. Generally this is achieved through the medium of developing insights and understanding through discussions, or dialogue. The effectiveness of counseling with the mentally subnormal has been examined by Stacey and De Martino.[6] Apparently results vary greatly, leading to the conclusion that counseling as a means of changing the life trajectory of the mentally subnormal depends to a very considerable degree on the training, skill and experience of the counselor. Such well-trained personnel are not readily available to all public schools. Since most teacher training institutions support a reinforcement approach to learning, this seems to be a determining reason to concentrate on this approach. Unfortunately, the choice is not a clear one. Having chosen the path of reinforcement, the positions presented by many different theorists must then be sifted for their appropriateness for this special population. Thus a theoretical basis for program planning must rely on a tenuous interpretation of rather debatable psychological learning theory.

The current state of learning theories is such that no firm basis for methodological presentation can be derived from any universally accepted theory. Even the adoption of an associationist position, whether it views learning as conditioning of responses, as the formation of connections between situation and responses, as drive reduction or as a cognitive system in which interaction of organism and environment, goals, patterns, insight and meaning are stressed, seems inadequate for our purposes. No one theoretical position seems able to provide a consistent framework from which to launch a methodological teaching pattern.

However, basic problems of motivation have been treated in an orderly manner by Maslow.[7] Although his model has not been validated with a mentally subnormal population, its eminent rationality recommends a brief discussion relative to the problem of developing a useful work-study program for mentally subnormal youth.

Prepotency needs

Behavior is determined by the environmental stimuli. It is, however, motivated by a hierarchy of needs generally working somewhat simultaneously (but to differing degrees of strength) to pre-empt the consciousness of the individual. Maslow, in discussing his theory of self-actualizing motivation, makes the point that the highest levels of personal development cannot occur in the absence of the satisfaction of basic needs. These he lists as the basic physiological needs, safety needs, belongingness and love needs, and esteem needs. Only after an individual has generally satisfied these needs or at least located sources which are available to him to satisfy these needs does the next level of unrest or need arise: that of self-actualization or doing those things he is capable of and interested in doing. To be free to develop his potential as a human being, he must have satisfied the basic needs: physiological, safety, belongingness and love, and esteem.

Basic to understanding the motivation of an individual is the prepotency operation of the needs. Under extreme conditions of deprivation, any one of the needs may so pre-empt the consciousness of an individual that none of the other needs exert an influence on his behavior. When a person is desperately hungry, he may "dream food, remember food, think about food, and emote only about food." All other needs may become simply nonexistent.

As basic needs are satisfied, their effect on behavior becomes less, thus freeing the individual to attend to other, less basic, needs. Since the educational program for the mentally subnormal is dependent upon the willingness of the learner to attend to the stimuli presented, it becomes mandatory that the youngsters have their basic needs at least partially satisfied. This probably implies that the school may need to provide food, warmth, protection, and belonging, *before* the teacher can hope to expect much attention from the youngsters to the stimuli which will help them learn the skills required for occupational adequacy. Furthermore, if the learner appears to be unmotivated in the classroom, it may be wise to inquire into his basic needs since he may be responding to a prepotent need of a pervasive sort which precludes his attending to higher level motives. In view of the large number of mentally subnormal youngsters who come from the lower socio-economic levels, it seems doubly important to be aware of the effect on behavior of the unsatisfied basic needs. As a corollary, behavior patterns which develop via the secondary reinforcement route to satisfy prepotent needs, add to the complication. Under conditions of chronic hunger, a youngster may concentrate almost exclusively on food. This may lead to stealing as a way of satisfying the need for food. The acts of stealing may then become reinforcing since they contribute to the reduction of the basic need for food. It is probably too much to hope that the school may compensate for deprivation in all the basic needs, yet an understanding of the pervasiveness of these needs, their relative prepotency at different times, and the importance of satisfying these basic needs before the learner can attend to the tasks set for him in the schoolroom or vocation situation, seems to be an essential for every teacher. As these affect the attempts to develop occupational adequacy in the mentally subnormal, so does the understanding of the mechanism of motivation become important.

All of the theories seem to have some common elements, and it would seem prudent to recognize these as a basis for methods. There seems to be in the aggregate some agreement that to be effective the learning situation should provide for the following principles.

1] Active participation is more effective than passive reception.

2] Responses during the learning process are modified by their consequences. Adequate knowledge of results is mandatory.

3] The learning situation must be realistic to the learner.

4] The learning process occurs through a wide variety of experiences unified around a central core of purpose.

5] Realistic goal setting leads to more satisfactory improvement than unrealistic goal setting and is dependent upon feedback.

6] Tolerance for failure is best taught through providing a backlog of success. *LEVEL OF ASPIRATION IS RAISED*

7] The realness of the conditions under which the learning takes place and the readiness of the learner, contribute to the integration of the learning products into the personality of the learner.

Other significant agreement areas have been identified by Burton;[8] however for purposes of this discussion, these seven principles seem to be important considerations in teaching the mentally subnormal. These can and should be provided in a high school program.

This group of students needs prevocational and vocational work experience. Any special curriculum should include part-time job training integrated with academic and social development skills followed by full-time, on-the-job experience which is supervised by a high school teacher or counselor. Essentially, the program should provide prevocational experience, job tryout, and actual job placement, all under school supervision.

This is not a new innovation for the educable mentally handicapped, but not many schools have extended their programs to include the whole range of the mentally subnormal. Some programs with work experience for educable mentally handicapped are based on the needs of the learner. The program has the advantage of being designed to fit the needs of the child rather than forcing the child to fit into the traditional high school program. In some cases it is a terminal program for youngsters of limited ability. For those who have the ability to benefit from a four-year program, it may include, in addition to academic subjects which would be used as tool subjects, something in the way of occupational information and job training in the school building; job placement outside the school is sometimes attempted. Too often job placement is for only four or five hours a day and is without supervision or counseling. It should be experience in which students work a full eight-hour shift supervised and guided by school personnel. Schools which have made an effort to coordinate school and work experiences have found this a highly successful approach.[9] However, there are not many programs of this kind being offered, and many of those which are offered are restricted by lack of system and support.

Curriculum needed

An effective high school learning situation for the mentally subnormal calls for exposure of the learners to tasks which, when learned, contribute to his occupational adequacy. In this consideration the skills which have been identified by research as being present to a significant degree in successfully employed mentally subnormal individuals, but lacking in the unsuccessful, should become the central curricular consideration.

In regard to intelligence the following have been established.

1] The magnitude of the I.Q. seems to be not so important as the efficiency with which the individual uses whatever abilities he has.

2] Above about a 2.5 grade level, academic achievement does not seem to be a critical factor in securing employment, but the ability to read, and write, communicate and perform arithmetic functions are limiting in terms of the level of employment for which an individual may qualify. Probably specific reading, writing, and arithmetic functions are more important to employability than general levels of achievement. These functions vary from job to job and may probably be taught without reference to supporting academic skills.

In regard to personal appearance, the following need attention:

1] correction of orthopedic handicaps by prosthetics and exercise
2] correction of cosmetic disfigurements if possible
3] correction of speech problems
4] development of habits of cleanliness
5] development of habits of good grooming

6] learning the skills of simple cooking and kitchen cleanliness

7] learning the skills of clothing cleanliness, repair, and renovation

8] learning habits of physical fitness and weight control

Socially, the following characteristics seem to be important.

1] Learning to get along with peers is an ability that may be demonstrated in a variety of ways. Social acceptance can be accomplished by being an active, participating member of a group. It might also involve being a social isolate: that is, a person who has no interaction with a group may be demonstrating perfectly good social behavior even though he has no part in group activities. So long as his presence does not interfere with the operations of the group, he is "getting along with his peers." The key to this skill seems to be his lack of interference rather than his degree of participation.

2] Learning to get along with supervisors can be demonstrated in a variety of ways. It is critical that he be willing to accept advice, supervision, or criticism without becoming aggressive, moody, withdrawn, or discouraged. Probably this ability is a product of his own "self-concept" and develops from a backlog of success experiences which allow him to accept both help and criticism without becoming discouraged.

3] Ability to work independently as a demonstration of maturity may be in part a function of chronological and mental age. It is also a reflection of his "self-concept." However, it seems more intimately a skill which can be learned if considerable practice of a successful nature is provided.

4] It is quite probable that the ability to work with a group is dependent upon a person's ability to work independently. Group work generally calls for the pooling of individual efforts in some kind of time sequence. It depends, therefore, on the meshing of a great many individual contributions. It would appear that this skill can be learned only after an individual has first learned to work independently. Then he may learn those skills of patience, timing, and co-ordination which are required for group activities.

5] Cheerfulness is a characteristic that reflects both an attitude and an individual's feeling of self-worth, and there is no reason to believe that an expression of optimism or cheerfulness cannot be at least partially taught. The accentuation of the positive is emphasized in the training programs of many kinds of service personnel (notably airline stewardesses) where the specifics of this behavior are judged to be important to the job. By careful attention to the use of praise, building up a backlog of successful experience, and emphasizing the benefits of a smiling countenance, such a public image may become habitual.

Vocational skills which are general and important in virtually all employment situations follow.

1] Skills of dexterity and co-ordination involve the assembly of both fine and gross, simple and complex units; sorting according to color, size, shape, and texture; and the simple and involved use of both hands and feet. These can, with practice, be successfully learned.

2] The ability to persist or stick to a repetitive or demanding task is a skill which can be taught and may become an important part of a prospective employee's vocational equipment.

3] The ability to work under varying conditions of pressure, time, noise, distraction, or supervision seems to be an important employee characteristic. Apparently practice and exposure to these conditions is crucial to its development.

4] Learning to be responsible for getting to and from the

job, being on time, being careful with property and other personnel, and being properly dressed or equipped for the job, seem critical to employment. Although chronological and mental maturity are certainly factors in this sense of responsibility, it is quite evident that elements of this characteristic can be learned.

5] Realistic job expectation seems to be largely a product of experience in both self-evaluation and job evaluation. It is both important and teachable.

The degree to which the intellectual, personal, social, and vocational skills interact to produce an employable individual vary from person to person and from job to job. The degree to which good skills in one area can compensate for poor skills in another also may vary in the same manner. Yet it seems the task of the school to provide the environmental milieu which will allow the fullest development of each of these skills in every individual and to attend to and evaluate progress in each specific skill. If after extensive evaluation, training, and experience an individual appears to still be deficient in one or some of these areas, employment may still be possible. This is dependent upon selective job placement so the job demands are not those in which the student is deficient. The training program should provide optimum conditions for personal development in each area, but the job placement activities should recognize that imperfect learning is often the rule rather than the exception.

Sequences of study

A sixteen-unit program is the planned requirement for graduation. A suggested class schedule is shown in Appendix A. This can be accomplished within the existing framework of the requirements of the usual high school program. Since four years of physical education participation are generally required by law and usually carry no credit, it is suggested that a health education class could be interspersed for two periods a week during the entire four years and could carry a total of one unit of credit for the four years. The health education classes can be taught in the special room for the handicapped by the special class teacher or by assigned personnel, and should be appropriate to the health problems for the handicapped. It should include grooming, rest, desirable health habits, and proper diet. The three physical education periods per week should be devoted to remedial physical activities for the handicapped individuals involved. Although no credit is ordinarily given for this activity it could become an important part of the total rehabilitation program as it will continue for the entire time that the student is enrolled in school. When possible, an orthopedic surgeon and a physical therapist should be consultants to the program.

During the first year the student should carry individual classes of academic subjects which carry one unit of credit each. These can be in social studies, reading, and mathematics; or possibly the student may be integrated into classes and courses offered in the regular high school program. Two periods per day during the freshman year should be used for vocational evaluation and testing, and two periods per day should be used for vocational orientation purposes. This is the Prevocational Evaluation. One-fourth credit should be given for each of these four periods during the freshman year. Thus the total number of credits which could be earned during the freshman year would be 4.25.

During the Sophomore and Junior years, the programs could be identical in that the student could spend half-time in class and half-time in job experiences (Job Tryout or Vocational Adjustment Training). It should be possible for each student during both the Sophomore and Junior years to have experience with a total of eight jobs as job tryout, or vocational adjustment training. One-fourth unit of credit should be given for each nine-week job experience. Only jobs which provide a minimum of two hours per day could be considered as satisfying this requirement. The occupation used would be of the type which the students will encounter when they seek competitive employment: namely, the service occupations, light industrial, and business and clerical types of jobs at an unskilled or semiskilled level.

During the Sophomore and Junior years the student should continue to carry two academic classes for one unit of credit each. These can be made appropriate to the needs and abilities of the student and should supplement the job tryout experience which they are receiving in the community. Academic classes in the sophomore and junior years should include such topics as job applications, social security, labor unions, and insurance. One unit of credit a year could be given for the vocational information course during the Sophomore and Junior years. During these two years, the total number of credits earned would be 4.25 per year for a total number of 8.5 credits: one for each course class, one-fourth for each year of health education, and one-fourth for each job experience.

During the Senior year the third phase of the program (Permanent Vocational Placement), physical education and health education should continue as in the previous three years. In addition, the student may choose to carry one or more other course. It is expected, however, that his major commitment would be to a job which employs him for at least four hours per day and preferably eight. For this experience the student may receive one-fourth unit of credit for the health education class, two credits for other courses, and two credits for the work experience for a total of 4.25 credits. Thus the four-year maximum total of credits which the students may be able to earn is 17.

A large majority probably would be able to earn the required 16 credits, and for some students it would be necessary to spend an extra period in school in order to meet the requirements for graduation. As a supplementary aid it may be possible for the student to get specific training in skills which will be encountered during the job experience. Classes which are typically offered may be in such trades as upholstery, metal work, carpentry, welding, typing, and cooking.

TIME SEQUENCE

Although this time sequence is presented in terms of a four-year program, it is entirely possible that any student may find it necessary to repeat the first-, second-, and third-, or fourth-year programs in order to develop the maturity in specific areas needed to make him employable. It is entirely conceivable that it could become even an eight-year program for some students.

Selection of students

The selection of students who can benefit from work experience provided by a high school program has been a baffling problem for many schools. In the examination of the characteristics which differentiated between the successful and unsuccessful clients of the Employment Evaluation and Training Project, some factors which might be thought to be significant proved to be unimportant. For example in the I.Q. range of 50 to 90, there seemed to be no difference in the employability. Second, above an academic achievement level of about 2.5 in arithmetic, reading, and language arts, there seemed to be no advantage in employability favoring those youngsters who had higher achievement levels. Third, so long as students are kept in the protected environment of the school until they are about nineteen or twenty years of age, their physical maturity will be at about an optimum for employment. Fourth, the mere presence of an ancillary handicap such as a speech problem, a vision problem, or an orthopedic disability did not seem to limit the likelihood of employment.

It would seem from this information that schools and other training programs could well afford to be quite flexible in

their use of these characteristics in their selection requirements. Furthermore, a record of good behavior in school does
not necessarily indicate a good probability for employment
after the youngsters have matured and left school. This is to
say that docility, which makes it possible for a youngster to
get along well in the classroom, may be the antithesis of
initiative. And, in employability, the showing of initiative is
an important aspect of the student's behavior. It follows that
it is the better part of prudence to allow students with records
of poor behavior in academic programs to become a part of
this vocationally oriented program. An error of commission
may be less costly than an error of omission.

Personnel

Although much of the academic part of the educational
program and also the training of skills for independent living
can be handled by one teacher in the classroom, it is recommended that a minimum of two teachers or one teacher and
one rehabilitation counselor be assigned to handle this program from the beginning. This has several advantages. Probably the most important is that as one teacher is providing
for the academic work and the skills of independent living in
the classroom the other may be investigating job placement,
supervising the students in work samples, or making contacts
with the business community to insure the acceptance of the
students as they are ready for job tryout or job placement.

This also allows for rotating the class so half are in the
academic and independent living part of the program in the
morning, and in the prevocational part in the afternoon while
the other half of the class reverses the order. Since the community becomes an extension of the school program, it is
important that there be a teacher whose duties are the co-
ordination of the community effort with the school program
as well as one in the school building itself. Therefore, during
the second year of the program an additional teacher is

needed. Also, if some of the students are to be integrated into the regular classes with other students, it is important that the liaison between the special program and the rest of the regular school program be provided. This cannot be done effectively if only one teacher is available to run the program. Such a liaison person must be free to visit the classes and interpret to the regular teachers needs and difficulties of the students who are being integrated in the regular programs in addition to searching for job placements.

However, with the two teachers it is possible to have as many as thirty youngsters in various training functions and under supervision. On the assumption that the students will be in different stages of their training and will be in many different places at different times, it is quite probable that no more than ten or fifteen may be in the classroom at any one time. Under ordinary circumstances and with programmed instruction in some of the academic areas, it is quite possible for the teacher who is in the homeroom to provide individual learning experiences for these students based on the needs as they have been demonstrated in the work situations. With each additional fifteen students, one more teacher will probably be needed. This is consistent with the usual standards suggested by state departments of public instruction.

Role of the Division of Vocational Rehabilitation Counselor

The first contact of the Division of Vocational Rehabilitation Counselor with the students should be in the freshman year. It should be possible for the Division of Rehabilitation counselor to provide the initial orientation to rehabilitation services through the Vocational Information course scheduled as a part of the regular school work. At this time the counselor will have an opportunity to become acquainted with the students, can be involved in the staffing, learn of special cases, and when students need services other than those available to accomplish his habilitation in the school, can make these arrangements. In most instances, the Division of Vocational Rehabilitation counselor is both willing and able to act as a consultant to the academic program. His years of counseling and vocational supervision are apt to have given him insights into the needs of the students in their vocational experiences not ordinarily shared by the school personnel. Furthermore, in this way he can become entirely familiar with the curriculum and will have an opportunity to suggest modifications which he thinks will be important to the habilitation of the students. During the entire duration of the student's program, the counselor should be apprised of the progress being made and the needs for special services in unique cases.

During the final stages of the student's program the counselor should become intimately involved, through job visitation, in watching the progress of the students. In this way the counselor will become aware of the needs for special services. He will know whether the student will be self-sufficient without further case referral or whether the student will need to be referred to other kinds of programs for additional training, such as apprenticeship training and the like.

If this involvement is started early, the Division of Vocational Rehabilitation counselor will become aware of "difficult" cases early in the career of the youngsters. He will have ample opportunity to plan for the appropriate services prior to the time the youngster finishes the school work. In addition, he will have had the opportunity to participate in curriculum planning and can make suggestions based on his experiences which would be appropriate to these difficult cases. While it is important for the school personnel to understand the role of the DVR counselor, it is equally important that the counselor become aware of the unique problems of the school personnel. This contributes to the overall effectiveness of the relationships between the school and the local agency.

Space requirements

Unless the school maintains an employment-sheltered workshop or a similar kind of facility, very little additional space other than that required for a double homeroom would be necessary. It should be kept in mind that during the time the students are engaged in prevocational evaluation, work samples from local industries should be available for practical experience and systematic observation of the work habits of the students. These require an additional amount of space other than that usually available in the regular classroom. Furthermore, centers for training in grooming and in simple cooking are a necessary part of this school program, and they may require additional room. The grooming space may require no more than the availability of a sink, a full-length triple mirror, and perhaps a small sewing corner. The modern Pullman-type kitchens are adequate for the simple cooking and cooking preparation required in this area of study. Thus, it is anticipated that a classroom not much larger than one and one-half to two times the size of the regular classroom could provide for the instruction of from thirty to sixty students. This is possible because the community is used as an extension of the school, and not more than thirty students would be in the classrooms at any one time.

While it is quite possible that a special corner for shop work may also be desirable, there seems to be no reason not to use the shop facilities which are a part of most schools and the home economics rooms which are available in the majority of high schools. However, the decisions to use these existing facilities or to have them in the special classroom should be up to the local school authorities, and may not necessarily be the same in all schools. In some schools the facilities may already be overtaxed and small individual units would therefore be called for. In others, scheduling difficulties may be insurmountable. Probably no set pattern will fit all situations, but the facilities for grooming, cooking, and evaluating must be provided, since they are vital components of the program.

A program for the small high school

Although the pattern of experiences described is appropriate for small as well as large high schools, in small schools with no special organization to provide for the needs of the mentally subnormal, it is probably best to concentrate on individual students rather than on groups. A guidance counselor, principal, or outstanding teacher might accept this responsibility.

In the academic area, an individual student may be integrated in whichever of the regular classes seems appropriate. His classroom work would probably need to be supplemented by remedial instruction of an individual nature. This could be done during homeroom period, study hall or after school. In this activity, the use of programmed instruction seems an excellent medium, first because it is systematic, and second because it makes minimal demands on the teacher's time.

A more difficult problem is that of providing meaningful work experience. While the tendency would be to provide this experience through jobs in the school, it seems more realistic to seek job experiences in the community. This can be done by soliciting the help of businessmen and/or farmers in the area who would be willing to become adjunct instructors to the school. The number and variety of jobs in which any student should be given experience would probably be different for each student, but a minimum of five different jobs would seem a good rule of thumb. Performance ratings should be used to record his progress, and no permanent job should be attempted until his record of work is satisfactory. Girls can be provided job experience in the same manner as boys. Hospitals, nursing homes, housekeeper duties, kitchen and restaurant aids have been good work placements for girls.

If a DVR counselor is located nearby, his help should be solicited as early as possible. He can indicate which of the services offered by his agency might be appropriate to the development of the student. More fundamentally, he is trained to do job placement. In this area, he is probably the most experienced professional available and can generally do a better job than can the school personnel. Furthermore, he can provide systematic follow-up supervision and advisement specifically related to work performance—a service badly needed by these students.

In the absence of a Division of Vocational Rehabilitation counselor, work placement can still be done by the school officials. Armed with the records of the work experience performance of the student, jobs which will allow the student to use his abilities in a meaningful manner should be sought. The procedure described in Chapter 4 is as appropriate in a small community as in a large city. Salesmanship is salesmanship in the country or in the city, but in either environment there is no substitute for enthusiasm, persistence, and commitment. *WHAT KIND OF SALESMANSHIP?*

4

A WORK PROGRAM
FOR THE MENTALLY SUBNORMAL

Principles of vocational development

THE vocational skills which seem to be important in the employability of the mentally subnormal were indicated in Chapter 2.

Unless specific practice in the development of these skills is provided under realistic conditions of immediate feedback and evaluation, it is probable that they will not be perceived by the student as being either pertinent or important. In addition, unless the learner has the opportunity to compare his performance and abilities with actual job demands, he probably will not make much progress toward developing a realistic vocational level of aspiration. Nor can he be expected to be able to make much of an effort to improve his performance, if he does not receive accurate and meaningful information on his strengths and his weaknesses relative to actual work. For these reasons this chapter is devoted to the systematic exploration of methods pertinent to the development of these skills throughout the entire secondary school career of the student.

As was indicated in Chapter 3, development of vocational skills proceeds through three stages: the prevocational evaluation stage, the vocational tryout stage, and the vocational placement stage. Not until a student meets an established level of competence at each stage should he be considered for the next stage of experience. Typically a student would be involved in prevocational evaluation during his first year, vocational tryout for the next two years, and vocational placement during his fourth year of school. However, a lack of progress or slow development could indicate the need for additional time in each stage. Thus an individual student may need as many as eight years to develop the maturity necessary for successful employment performance. Since the goal of the secondary program is the development of an employable person, the exact amount of time needed to develop these skills to an acceptable level need not be viewed as an important consideration.

Prevocational evaluation phase

The first experience of the student with the world of work should be under conditions which will provide the opportunity for him to evaluate his abilities as a worker and to learn in detail the requirements of what is involved in a work situation. For this reason the vocational information periods and the vocational evaluation periods should give the student experience with work situations which are realistic in nature. It has been very common in some schools to provide the students with experience in working at jobs in the school: cafeteria, food service line, janitorial work, and experience of contact with the world of work by using work samples from local industries in a school operated workshop, or through services from an already established workshop run by an outside agency (*See* Chap. 6).

Work samples

Many privately operated workshops have used work samples as a source of different kinds of tasks that can be used for evaluative purposes in their workshop setting. In some cases they have used work samples from their own subcontract work for work skill evaluation. In this aspect of the students' training it is recommended that the same procedure be followed except that it be in the public schools.

Virtually any industry is willing to give work samples to the schools for the purpose of developing people who could become a part of their labor force after they have received their training. Generally speaking, the industries will have typical samples of work which they require of their employees. These can be secured by visiting the personnel or shop manager. At the same time that the work sample is secured, the teacher should get the production standards for this particular job so that the students can find out how their production performance compares with that of the workers in industry. It is suggested that the teacher work out a table to show what per cent of normal the production of any student may represent.

The teacher should secure enough work samples so that one work station for each student in the classroom will be available. Furthermore, the work samples should be chosen in such a way that they provide a wide variety of kinds of performance by the student. Work samples which require the student to estimate such things as quantity, size, speed, and quality should be selected. Work samples which require the exercise of memory for oral directions and memory for written directions are necessary. Work samples requiring the reading of addresses, sales orders, patterns, and directions should be included. Samples which require counting, adding, subtracting, multiplying, dividing, measuring, using fractions, sales slips, invoices, or involvement in production costs should also be used. Skills of writing whether listing items, keeping production records, completing sales orders, or information to be read by others, should be included where possible. The work samples should include those which require strength of hands, arm strength, back strength, dexterity of fingers, hands, arms, feet and legs for both speed and accuracy, eye-hand co-ordination, eye-hand-foot co-ordination, and co-ordination of both hands.

The object of all of the evaluation is to provide as many different experiences in skills for the students as they might run into in the unskilled and semiskilled tasks in industrial situations. Under most conditions each job sample will have a variety of requirements. It will call for the use of many of the listed skills in different quantities at different times. These are excellent kinds of work experiences for the students and provide a realistic medium for making the kinds of evaluation which will help determine the strengths and the weaknesses of this student for program planning purposes.

Rate of pay

An important consideration in the use of the job samples from industry is the determination of a rate of pay for the students in the classroom. Although there are many values to be gained from pay, among the most important is that which is pertinent to the general motivation of the students. If the students are given the opportunity to earn money for the work which they do, it is one of the best ways to impress upon them the value of developing good work habits. The actual amount of pay should depend upon the rate of pay which a worker in industry receives for the same job. That is, if the job pays at the rate of a dollar an hour for 300 units of work, the student in school should be paid on a similar basis. If he does only half of a number of units, he would receive half the basic hourly rate. Also, it is perfectly logical to set a base rate which is less than a worker in industry might get. For example, if the school felt that it can pay only 50¢ an hour for the number of units ordinarily calling for $1.00 in pay, then the same ratio of units to hourly wage should apply except that the top pay would be 50¢ rather than $1.00.

It is extremely important that students be given an opportunity to earn some money from the very beginning. If the school feels that it cannot pay the students for this kind of work, it is sound to solicit money from service clubs such as Kiwanis, Lion's, Rotary, Optimist, and Exchange, or to use money from the P.T.A. to pay for this kind of experience. It could be considered that the wages paid to the students for their job sample work is a necessary part of the educational expense of the program, and should be budgeted for as are other expenses such as textbooks and paper.

While this may be foreign to the thinking of many school people, it is a necessary part of the training and has been used in sheltered workshops to very good advantage for many years. There seems to be no logical or philosophical reason why the payment cannot be considered a part of the expense of operating the program in the school, since it is such a vital force for motivation.

Production records

A careful record of the productivity of each student, including the job which he has been working on, his production rate, the rate of pay of the job, and the amount of pay that he actually earns, should be kept on a daily basis. In addition, it becomes the job of the teachers to estimate the quality of the work completed by the student, his reaction to supervision, his relations with his co-workers, his general work attitudes, his assets and liabilities as a worker, and whether he is improving, regressing, or remaining static in the development of his qualities as a worker. In this evaluation his ability to get along with his peers, his ability to get along with his supervisor, his ability to work independently, his ability to work with groups, his cheerfulness, his dexterity, his persistence, his adjustment to pressure, his sense of responsibility, and his job satisfaction should all be included in the progress report. An example of this kind of report is shown in Appendix B. These should be summarized at the end of each week, so that a systematic record of his progress can be made. Appendix C is an example of this summary report.

The evaluation report then becomes a basis for planning his experience program so that the areas in which he has shown evidences of weaknesses will be given additional emphasis to allow him to develop the kinds of work habits which will, over a period of time, make him employable. Furthermore, the progress sheets can become the source of discussion in the classroom periods devoted to employment information. Since the jobs themselves are samples of jobs which come from specific industries, the realism of relating student performance to what would be required to hold jobs in a particular industry, adds to the meaningfulness of the tasks that they are performing. With the addition of the pay on a weekly basis, the realism becomes quite evident.

Job surveys

One of the most common difficulties encountered in working with mentally subnormal youth in a vocational program is their lack of familiarity with the jobs which are available whose requirements are within their abilities. Investigators who have worked in the field, such as Erdman,[1] have reported on the lack of realism of the job expectations of the mentally subnormal. Yet this is one of the most important of the kinds of learning necessary if an individual is to become employed. For that reason, it is recommended that the job analyses in the community be done not by the teacher alone but by the students and teacher in the pre-vocational phase as a part of their regular school work.

Approximately once each month the whole class should prepare a job analysis of one job in the community. The form in Appendix D is illustrative of the kind of information which should be secured about the job.

When the survey group returns to the classroom, it is then

possible for each individual to rate himself in terms of how well his abilities may fit the requirements of the job. He can indicate, for example, whether or not he prefers clerical, sales, agricultural, or some other classification of jobs. He can rate himself as to whether or not he has the experience required for this particular kind of a job. He may take the employment service tests of the company-made tests necessary for this particular kind of job. He can examine himself to see whether he has the driver's license, health certificate, or other kind of special permit required for the job. Requirements of union membership may be an item for consideration.

The investigating of sources which provide labor, the employment service, the use of help-wanted ads, the labor union, or the making of voluntary applications can be explored. The importance of the labor supply for this particular kind of job may help him to decide whether this is a good or poor job to apply for. The kinds of practices used in paying the employees and the amount of money paid to the employee can become a source of discussion. The degree to which the employee must work alone or work with others and environmental conditions, such as heat, cold, dampness, noise and so forth, under which he must work, can help him decide whether or not he can stand an inside or an outside job. The physical requirements of the job including those of sitting or standing, lifting, moving about, the requirements in terms of discrimination of form, color, size, and weight and the responsibility which the employee has had for handling money may also be included in the discussions.

To the degree that formal education is required for a job, the prospective employee-student will have an opportunity to compare his education level against that required. He may also be interested in finding out what kinds of things are given in a training program which may be connected with the job. He may then be concerned about how much reading, arithmetic, or speaking is required and whether he can perform those functions to the degree required by the job. If it is possible to get a work sample from the particular job or industry visited or a description of the work from the survey for, the student may then try out his performance against that which is considered standard for a normal employee in the job. He may then have a chance to evaluate whether he can change as the situation may require, or meet the amount of pressure or stress of the job. The degree of direction, and the kind of supervision provided can be discussed.

He may then have an opportunity to examine himself in terms of the actual requirements of the job such as the need to estimate quantity, size, speed or quality. His responsibility for the safety of physical facilities, the safety of others, or his own safety and the various threats to safety of this particular job can be identified. He may then have an opportunity to find out whether the strength of his hands, arms, legs, or back are appropriate to the requirements of the job. Finally he would have an opportunity to judge his own co-ordination of eye-hand, eye-hand-foot, or both hands as they are related to the particular requirements of this job.

As a corollary, employment application forms can be collected when the job analysis is done, and these can be used in the arithmetic and reading lessons to help with the preparation of the individual for the actual job application.

Counseling of the mentally subnormal

A study of the literature indicates that the degree to which the mentally subnormal responds to counseling, either of an individual or group nature, varies considerably. The reports are quite consistent in indicating that great difficulties are encountered in the development of insights from counseling procedures with the mentally subnormal. It is here suggested that counseling can be effective, if it is made specific to a particular job situation, and if this specificity is related to the actual abilities of the client as demonstrated in job analysis and individual analysis. That is to say, the student's understanding of his limitations and assets, when they are specific to the requirements of a specific job, will become meaningful to him. Indeed, it is only under these conditions that these youngsters apparently learn what they can and cannot do. Even the actual experience of working on the job does not seem to provide them with the insights necessary for realistically evaluating their abilities and disabilities. The desired insights occur only when the specific elements that are required by the job, such as the reading level, arithmetic computations, and physical strength are compared with their own. *CONCRETE*

Advisement and guidance of the mentally subnormal seems to be a very specific kind of operation. In order to be effective the individual abilities and disabilities of the clients must be objectively demonstrated and related to known job requirements. This should not be construed to suggest that there is no place for group discussions, role playing, attempts to achieve insight and understanding of other kinds of problems. It does mean, however, that the attempts at any kind of counseling should proceed first from specific, objective, and easy to understand information in order that the individual will have the insights which will allow him to appraise his abilities and disabilities in a realistic manner. Only when he has this information firmly in mind, can he turn his attention to the development of those skills necessary for a specific kind of job performance. Training is therefore based on precise information of the exact requirements of a particular job and the degree to which he falls short of meeting those requirements.

Other considerations

It should be obvious that other kinds of information are also necessary for the prospective employee. He should be aware of such things as the problems and laws regarding wages, the responsibilities of employers and employees, knowledge about labor union membership requirements, and the advantages and disadvantages of union membership, information having to do with the withholding tax, group insurance policies, vacations and vacation pay, sick leave and sick leave pay, minimum pay schedules, workmen's compensation laws, and so on. This information may be obtained from any employment service office and can be used as a part of the general program of occupational information. It should not take the place or supersede the use of materials which have been obtained from the job analyses, the job production records on the job samples, or the occupational information part of the program.

It is also recommended that during this time the counselor in the local Division of Vocational Rehabilitation be brought in as a resource individual to explain to the students the use of the Division of Vocational Rehabilitation counselor and allowing them to benefit from the information which he has for them, but it also gives the counselor the opportunity to meet the students prior to the time that they may become eligible for employment. It will also give him an opportunity to begin to work on various corrective programs which may be necessary before these particular students become employable.

Summary of prevocational phase

Materials for prevocational evaluation and information should come from the community itself. In the absence of a school operated or community operated sheltered workshop, businesses and industries should be solicited for work samples. At the same time liberal use should be made of production standards, and other instructional materials such as application forms, bulletin board notices, descriptions of job conditions, and brochures explaining job benefits from businesses in the community. The students should use job samples or workshops for their initial work experience, and they should be paid by the school or the workshop for their performance.

The teacher and the students should make a job analysis at least once each month. The students should then use the job analysis form for self-analysis relative to the actual demands of the job.

Academic work should be tied to the jobs through the use of the materials solicited from the businesses and modified by a knowledge of academic demands as revealed by the job analyses. In this way the entire prevocational experience is intimately related to future job experiences and work performance is rewarded with money earned. Thus the school actually supplies the first employment experience for the student. It is on a kind of work which has its roots in the community and is performed under conditions having less stress than those of the actual job.

Job tryout phase
Vocational adjustment training

The primary goal of the job tryout phase of the program is to give the students experience in working in different kinds of jobs for a controlled period of time. It is recommended that a student be placed on each job for a minimum of two months during this part of his program. Thus in the course of a school year the student would have approximately two months' experience on each of four different jobs. Jobs in the light industrial, general service, food service, and business areas should be sought. The program should include placement in grocery stores, cafeterias, carpenter shops, hospitals, rest homes, furniture stores, cleaning and pressing shops, warehouses, upholstery shops, cafes, drugstores, hardware stores, and any other business which may offer the conditions desired for employment of mentally subnormal persons. In the job tryout phase of the program, the businessmen in the community actually become an extension of the school program. The selection of the jobs for job tryout or vocational adjustment training should be made with the end in view that these jobs will be used by all the students on a rotating basis. Therefore, none of the business places should be looked upon as offering permanent employment. They should be chosen for the variety of experiences which they can give to the students and for the different kinds of supervision and working experiences they provide. By using the job analysis form referred to previously, it should be possible to get a selection of jobs that will give students the opportunity to work both inside and outside, under varying conditions of temperature, moisture, and noise, or where there are unpleasant odors, irritating dust and dirt, or any of a variety of job conditions.

Role of the employer

Of critical importance is the attitude of the employer. It should be possible to put the student under working conditions in which he will be exposed to various kinds of employer reactions, ranging from benign, accepting supervision to demanding and fairly harsh supervision. In this part of the program it is extremely important that the school instructor, who is to do the supervision in the community, work very closely with the employers. He can secure their co-operation in providing the greatest variety of working conditions and demands that the community has to offer. In this way an adequate evaluation of the student can be made so that, when the time comes for him to be placed on a permanent job, a job may be picked which will be most suitable to his abilities and which will not penalize him for his disabilities.

No job tryout or vocational adjustment training position should be selected which does not allow for a full half-day of employment for the student. By using half-day positions, it is possible to provide for two groups of students since half of them will be in the school during the morning while the other half are on the jobs in the community and in the afternoon the two groups are reversed. Furthermore, this reduces by half the number of work stations needed for the students. It is expected that under this scheme, fifteen work stations will provide the experiences for thirty students. Thus, if the program runs for two years, it is expected that no more than thirty work stations would be needed to provide for sixty students.

The role of employers as adjunct teachers in this program is critical. Unless the employers are willing to take a different pair of students every two months, they probably should not be considered for this phase of the program. Furthermore, there is often a very great tendency for the employers not to provide a realistic work situation. They are apt to bend over backwards in trying to help the students to be successful when, as a matter of fact, their primary job is to provide for the evaluation and not for success experience as such. Whether a student becomes successful in his job tryout experiences is the joint responsibility of the teacher and the student, not the employer. It is the employer's task to provide a realistic work situation which provides the kind of experience needed for an honest evaluation of the capabilities of the student.

Role of the work co-ordinator

Of critical importance is the evaluation of the progress of the student on each of the jobs which he will have experience with in this phase of the program. The same evaluation form used in prevocational experience which includes a progress report is one that has been found to be very helpful. It provides for evaluation in the personal and social areas and also in the work habit and efficiency areas and asks the employer to indicate whether the student is improving with experience. This makes it possible for the co-ordinator and the classroom teacher to work together in the development of experiences within the classroom which will add to the maturity level of the student in the particular areas in which he may be deficient. In other words, it provides a basis for program planning.

Roughly to the degree that the school co-ordinator shows interests in the progress of his students, so also will the businessman-employer be concerned with the experiences which he is providing for the students. It becomes mandatory, therefore, that the school co-ordinator visit with each employer at least one day each week to supervise the students and to work with the employer in the evaluation of the student's progress, Typically, a co-ordinator can be responsible for the job stations in fifteen different jobs employing thirty students on a half-day each basis. Should the number of work stations and the number of students served become larger than this, an additional co-ordinator is needed for each thirty students. An additional classroom teacher should be employed for each new group of thirty students.

Rate and use of pay

Perhaps one of most critical of the aspects of the job tryout or vocational adjustment training phase of the program becomes one of pay for the student in training. It is recommended that the employer pay each student a minimum of 50¢ per hour for average work, 25¢ per hour for below average work and 75¢ per hour for above average work. Thus the pay of the student is commensurate with that for any individual who is in a training program, but at the same time it is geared to an evaluation of the kind of job which he is doing. In some communities an average of 50¢ per hour is probably more than some of the business people may wish to pay. Although individual adjustments probably will need to be made on a local basis, it has been found to be a good rule of thumb that if the employer is not willing to invest his money at this modest rate, he probably should not be included as a part of the training program.

Criterion for performance

The criteria for deciding when a student is working at a level which would indicate that he is a candidate for permanent employment cannot be specifically determined. However, a reasonable standard is that unless the student is average or above in two-thirds of the characteristics evaluated on the employers' evaluation sheet, he probably should be continued in the program of vocational adjustment training for a longer period of time. When he demonstrates average or above average performance on more than two-thirds of the characteristics indicated in the employers' evaluation sheet, he is a good prospect for permanent job placement. For many of the students this level of performance will be achieved in the two-year-period allotted for this experience. For a small percentage (perhaps one-fourth of the students) one year or less experience will be enough to judge their capabilities. These students could be moved to a permanent job placement without further training. For an additional 25 per cent of the students, it is probably necessary that a third or even a fourth year of vocational adjustment training be engaged in prior to the time they will have developed the maturity to be placed in competitive employment. Once again, the goal of the program is the development of an employable individual, and time, therefore, should not become an interfering consideration.

Finding work tryout jobs

In seeking employers who would be willing to let their business be used as an extension of the school program, it has been found that a "door-to-door selling" approach is very effective. Whether this is done on a friendship basis or whether the employer can be convinced that it is important for him to aid the schools in the jobs which they are trying to do in the development of employable personnel is not

particularly important. Of critical importance is the willingness of the employer to accept the supervision of the school
in the operation of his business, and provide daily employment for at least two students for two months and then two
new students for the next two months. He must be willing to
make his business an adjunct to the school program.

In some communities service clubs have helped the schools
to find job tryout stations. The Excaliber Club of Lansing,
Michigan has an "operation bird-dog." This is a permanent
part of their service activities and is run by a continuing
committee of club members who scout for jobs in behalf of
the mentally retarded.[2] This has been found to be a very
effective system for finding both permanent jobs and positions for job tryout training. Furthermore, it has the advantage of adding the prestige of the organization to the
school program thus practically assuring community understanding and acceptance. However, unless the school co-
ordinator works carefully and systematically with the service
club members involved, they are apt to secure inappropriate
jobs for the students in the program. There is sometimes a
tendency to overestimate the capabilities of the students
which can lead to serious consequences in the nature of
inappropriate student placement and misrepresentation to
the community. When well organized and informed, the
service club members are a boon to the program.

Permanent placement
Supervised vocational placement

A great many studies of the post school adjustment of
the mentally subnormal and the mentally retarded indicate
that the probability is excellent for successful community
adjustment of a very large percentage of these students. However, such studies are consistent in indicating that unless a
systematic effort at finding job placements for these students
after they have advanced beyond school age are provided,

the initial employment experience is apt to be haphazard and unsatisfactory. Generally, it is reported that the first year of employment opportunity for these former students is likely to be marked by a good deal of sporadic employment with frequent changes of jobs and discharges. This pattern for many is apt to continue until some responsible agency or individual makes a pronounced effort to find a job suitable to the abilities and the disabilities of the individual concerned.

Many school programs have profited from providing systematic efforts at job placements for their students. This has been successfully followed in many parts of the country, but it is perhaps most evident in the Lansing, Michigan program. On a state-wide basis, the State Division of Vocational Rehabilitation in Texas recently entered into a co-operative program with the public schools of the state. The Division now provides, on a co-operative basis, job co-ordinators and supervisors assigned to specific school systems for the placement of the youngsters in the Special Education program who are in need of and ready for job placement.[3] This very imaginative program is reported to have resulted in the job placement and case closures for over 600 former special education students during the year of 1963. It is anticipated that in 1964 this number will exceed 1,000. The officials in charge of the program are confident that the success of the program has now been demonstrated since a demand for counselor-work-placement supervisors has mushroomed.

Certainly, programs such as the Texas and Lansing programs should be considered for their appropriateness to other school systems. If provision can be made to secure the co-operation of the Division of Vocational Rehabilitation Counselor in the local area, this highly skilled individual can be of great help to the school system. Further, if it is possible to secure the co-operation of one or several of the service clubs in a community, such as that provided by the Excaliber Club of Lansing, Michigan or the Kiwanis Clubs in Kent County,

Michigan, this enhances the operation and often provides an entry into businesses and industries which would be closed to the local school personnel under ordinary circumstances.[4] In the absence of these kinds of cooperative arrangements, it still becomes the responsibility of the school to provide for the permanent work placement of each student as he satisfactorily completes the program.

Finding permanent jobs[5]

While the techniques employed by the school job placement supervisor may differ from community to community, the basic factor is to sell the prospective employer on the desirability of the graduates of the program as employees. This can be enhanced by using the complete record of the student's production, job experiences during his job tryout or vocational adjustment phase of the training, and the reports from employers who have the student in their businesses during the job tryout experiences. Thus, the school placement supervisor can point to the experiences of the student during his training program and to the kinds of evaluations which fellow employers have concerning the strengths and weaknesses of the student.

One of the most critical aspects in the attempt to secure employment for these students is that of the approach used with the prospective employer. It has been reported in many studies that the subject of mental subnormality should not be brought into the discussion unless it is absolutely necessary to do so. Typically the approach is one of encouraging the employer to accept a youngster who is not academically inclined but who has a record of good experience in the training program and who will be a good employee. The fact of whether he is or is not mentally subnormal need not be mentioned since the employer is interested in what the young person can do and not in whether he has scored low on an intelligence test. Although usually the jobs would be at an unskilled or semiskilled level, actual placements may range in complexity from jobs in which the employee is constantly supervised to those in which the individual is expected to be pretty much on his own. Occasionally some employees may even be responsible for some aspect of the business such as shipping, saleswork, or auto body painting and repair.

Two problems become critical in the search for employment. The first is that the individual should not be placed in a job where the academic demands either in reading, writing, arithmetic, or speaking are going to be greater than those which he can demonstrate. The second major consideration is that he not be placed in a job where it is understood that with increased seniority he may be placed in a more responsible position, and may have the welfare of other people, work schedules, production records, or the like as his responsibility. It becomes extremely important that the work placement be made with the clear understanding with the employer that the probability of advancement for the specific individual being employed is not great. When this is clearly understood, negotiations for actual job placement may be begun.

In many instances jobs which require labor organization membership are ruled out because of the seniority rules. It should be cleared with the labor business agents in the local area that placement for these particular individuals could be made on a limited membership basis so that the students would not become involved in the difficulties which could result from promotions based primarily on seniority rather than on a demonstration of specific skills.

The key to successful placement is finding the job commensurate with the characteristics and abilities of the person to be placed. Placement is apt to be successful if the placement counselor explores the possibility for placement within the community first, then places a student who has characteristics which most closely fit the requirements of the job. The major task of the placement counselor is a systematic survey of all the employment opportunities which seem to be suitable for the students he represents. It is not necessary for him to wait until the students are ready for placement; there will be no delay because the jobs which they might do have already been identified. A second advantage is that this will provide many opportunities to prepare prospective employers for their new employees without the pressure for immediate placement—a way of developing employment opportunities.

Fundamentally, this is a salesmanship job. As in any good selling, there are certain procedures which are basic regardless of what the product may be.

The first prerequisite for a good salesman is for him to know himself well. He should be aware of the kind of appearance that he makes, how his voice affects other people under differing conditions, what his desirable traits and what his undesirable traits may be. With this knowledge of himself he can then decide which of several approaches may be the most likely to succeed. If he does not possess a desirable "telephone voice," for example he should avoid making his first contact by telephone. On the other hand, if he does not present a pleasing appearance, it may be that his best approach is by introduction from someone known by the prospective employer so that the acceptance of his first visitation will carry the halo of being a friend of a friend of the employer.

A second characteristic of a good salesman is his knowledge of the product that he is selling. A thorough acquaintance with the history of the program, the methods of training, the characteristics of the youngsters in the program, the sequence of experiences, and the history of each youngster's development is absolutely vital. Unless the placement person is thoroughly acquainted with the program and with all the youngsters in the program, he should not attempt to seek job opportunities.

A third characteristic of a good salesman is his knowledge of the motives which could prompt a prospective employer to offer employment to these students. In this instance, a thorough knowledge of the company and the employer being approached is important. It is equally important, however, that reasons for hiring people who are atypical, which will make sense to an employer, be firmly in mind. The Employer's Mutual Insurance Co. of Wausau, Wisconsin, distributes a pamphlet entitled "Who Are the Handicapped?" This little pamphlet contains persuasive arguments for hiring handicapped individuals because of their stability, the pride which they take in their work, and their demonstration of ability to master their own problems despite being personally disadvantaged in comparison with other people. Many other reasons can be given, but essentially, the sales pitch is "the man more capable of solving his employer's problems is the man who has solved his own."

A fourth consideration involves the ability to handle objections. A good salesman will anticipate what the objections of a prospective employer may be and will have ready-made answers which he can present for each of the objections as they are presented. It is extremely important that the placement counselor, when an objection is brought up, answer as fully as he can with the information that is available to him.

The fifth characteristic of a good salesman is that of closure. Every interview should close with some statement of positive action. This may range from a promise to call on the employer at some future time to a promise to bring a student down for a job tryout. At the very least, a good placement counselor would not leave without getting a promise of the opportunity to do a job analysis in the company. In all of these closures there is the "foot in the door" technique which does not close without a promise of possible future participation of some kind.

One final characteristic of a good salesman is persistence. No matter how cool the reception, no matter how sharp the rebuff, a good salesman will continue to make calls despite seemingly overwhelming resistance. He knows that just on probability alone, the more calls he makes the greater his chances of being successful. There is too much at stake in job placement to let the difficulties scuttle the efforts.

Supervision on permanent jobs

During the first few weeks or months after placement of an individual on a new job, it should be the responsibility of the placement supervisor to visit him at least weekly and to assess the progress which the student is making on the job. Any problems, whether they are those of a vocational or personal and social nature, can be then worked out by the placement supervisor and by the student before they become devastating to vocational placement. The Lansing, Michigan system has established the rule that when an individual completes one year of successful employment he then becomes eligible to receive a high school diploma from their school system. This has several advantages, but the most important one is that of providing a goal toward which the individual can work, and giving the school the responsibility for the supervision of the student during his first year of actual work. While the precise rule of "one year of successful work experience" prior to the granting of a high school diploma may not be applicable in every school system, it seems very important that the first few weeks or months of the individual's job placement be under very careful supervision by the school and that the school feel a responsibility for this part of the program. This is one phase of the total school program and therefore requires as much if not more supervision than other phases of the program.

During this year of placement, it may be necessary for the student to be enrolled in evening classes designed to resolve specific problems he faces on the job. This should be arranged by the school, and the credit earned should be counted toward the graduation requirements.

5

AN ACADEMIC PROGRAM
FOR THE MENTALLY SUBNORMAL

IT is clear from the studies by Kennedy, Phelps, and Baller and Charles[1] that critical factors in the vocational success of mentally subnormal people are their personal and social skills. This work-study program is designed so that these skills are developed through both the work aspects of the program and also during the study aspects of the program. The half day of academic experience in school while the student is also actively engaged in work either of a pre-vocational sort (i.e., the performance on work samples or in a sheltered work situation or in the school created jobs) or in the vocational adjustment phase of the program (i.e., the half day of work in various semi-competitive employment situations in the community) is designed to provide for personal and social development as well as academic development. The integration of the academic, vocational, and personal and social characteristics can be accomplished by concentrating either on the work aspects or on the study aspects of the program. Chapter 4 was devoted to the work-experience aspects of the program. The present chapter is devoted to the study aspects of the program.

The study program

HOMEROOM

One of the critical elements for maintaining the interest of the mentally subnormal youngsters in the school situation is their acceptance by and integration with other students in the school system. For this reason it is strongly recommended that where a homeroom system is used, the mentally subnormal youngsters be assigned to homerooms in the same manner as are other students in the school. In this way the first period of the day, or the homeroom period, is spent in the planning of parties, discussion of manners and ethics, and consideration of responsible school behavior with the other students. This gives them a sense of being a part of the total school program. As the homeroom period ends and the students are dismissed to go to their other classes, mentally subnormal youngsters can then pass to their special classroom or to their work programs in the same manner that other students go to attend shop or physical education or their academic classes. It is extremely important that this integration of the subnormal students into the homeroom programs not be ignored. It seems to be one of the very critical aspects of the entire program, and it may make the difference between the willingness of the students to remain in the school even though they are in a special kind of program and their insistence upon dropping out. A sense of belongingness must not be denied these students.

It is equally important that the students in this program have the opportunity whenever possible to be integrated with other students in the various academic classes.

Critical to this integration is the attitude of the regular teachers. They should treat these youngsters as regular class members and not single them out for special attention or for ridicule. Teachers who display this acceptance attitude should be approached before the scheduling of a mentally subnormal youngster in their classes. Quite often regular class teachers are reluctant or fearful about accepting the mentally subnormal youngsters in their classes. In some cases a friendly chat over a cup of coffee can dispel these fears, but whatever reaction is anticipated from the teacher, the initial contact should be kept informal and tentative until some evidence of the teacher's attitude is apparent. An explanation of the behavior they can expect from a particular youngster may be all that is required. With other teachers it may be necessary to go into a more detailed discussion of the nature, causes, and consequences of mental deficit. Often the suggestion of a trial placement will bring about the desired cooperation. It should be recognized that for a variety of reasons some teachers simply will not accept these youngsters, and if that is the reaction, a strategic retreat is the only possible recourse.

PHYSICAL EDUCATION

Certainly one of the important kinds of activities in which many of these students can engage is physical education. To whatever extent it is possible, it is highly desirable to arrange for integration in the physical education activities of the school. This is especially true in school systems with programs in leisure-time activities, such as golf, tennis, swimming, bowling, fly-fishing, and the like. Furthermore, just the act of engaging in physical activity with the rest of the students in the school may foster friendship—friendship based on what the students can do as people rather than the kinds of academic progress which they may make. What this does to the development of their self-concept and concomitantly to the development of good personal and social behavior characteristics is immeasurable.

Since mentally subnormal youngsters are often inferior in their physical as well as in their personal skills, one of the much neglected activities which could contribute to the development of both kinds of skills is ballroom dancing. To teach these youngsters not only how to dance but also how to behave in such social situations contributes both to their physical co-ordination, their sense of rhythm, and the opportunity to be responsible for and concerned with the activities of another person—in this situation a dancing partner. It also gives them the opportunity to learn to dance in a manner which will be acceptable to their peers. It is difficult to estimate how important it may be for them to feel that they are acceptable in a social-dance situation and that they do not have to be judged by their lack of academic ability; therefore, it is recommended that if special tutoring sessions in dancing skills and in appropriate social behavior in social-dance situations is indicated, it be provided for these youngsters. It seems important to exploit any area which may contribute to their acceptance by their peers and to their own self-concept of acceptability, and this appears to be an activity which lends itself to the development of both.

DRIVER TRAINING

Since the difference between being employed or not being employed often depends on an individual's ability to get himself to and from the work situation, it seems important to consider driver training as a critical aspect of training. To the degree that it is possible to integrate the youngsters in the work-study program in a driver training program, this probably should be done. Once again, it is important to recognize that the mentally subnormal youngster will probably not master the skills of either an intellectual or a physical nature which are necessary to make him a safe driver in the usual period of time. Therefore, it is important that the special class teacher obtain the materials from the driver training instructor which are necessary for the academic part of driver training and present these materials to the special class students at a speed and in such a way that mastery can be assured. For the physical skills of driving, it is probable that up to twice as much instruction will be needed for their mastery by the mentally subnormal. In this case it is well to remember that the ability to drive a car safely and effectively may be a critical employment skill. It follows that the added time necessary for teaching this skill is well worth investing. If it is necessary to spend one or two or even three years on the actual instruction of driving for the mentally subnormal youngsters, then so be it. However, these youngsters should be given a chance to pass or fail the tests at the same time the other students take the tests so they will not appear to be getting preferential treatment. Subjecting them to the same time schedule as the other students may contribute to a high failure rate at the time of the initial test. The good which can be gained by not giving them differential treatment is well worth the failure. In any case, driving should be considered an extremely important and critical skill which must be taught to the mentally subnormal youngsters.

Sequence planning

It should be clearly kept in mind that the study aspects of the program follow the same curricular outline as the work aspects of the program. That is to say, the material to be taught in the study aspects of the program should be divided into the three basic levels of prevocational, vocational adjustment, and placement. The general definition of the levels are as indicated previously:

1] PREVOCATIONAL—students able to participate in sheltered, supervised, and semi-competitive work environments for a portion of each school day, but who by nature of their handicap or age are not eligible for vocational adjustment placement

2] VOCATIONAL ADJUSTMENT OR WORK TRYOUT—students who have demonstrated a sufficient degree of work and social and personal skills to become eligible for part-time competitive work placement on selected jobs in the community

3] PLACEMENT—students who are capable of performing work at a minimum competitive level and who have completed the general academic requirements for graduation from the work study program.

The students in the latter classification will be allowed to work for the entire school day but will have the supervisory, teaching, and advisement services of the program available to them as needed. At least one evening per week should be devoted to a school program which would deal with the immediate academic, personal, and social problems which they may encounter on a job.

PREVOCATIONAL INFORMATION

During the prevocational phase of the program, the job classification sheet should be the principle source of vocational information. The monthly job analysis mentioned in the preceding chapter should be continued as well as the self-analysis which permits the student to become increasingly aware of the demands that employment will place upon him and the particular problems which he, personally, will have to face in order to qualify for employment. As he becomes familiar with his own capacities in relation to the job, he should be able to demonstrate a better kind of judgment as to which jobs he thinks he might be able to perform within the community.

In addition to the job analysis sheets, guest speakers from the employment agency, from the Division of Vocational Rehabilitation, from the local labor unions, and from other agencies within the community could be used to answer questions which arise as a result of the studies of the functions of these agencies by the students. At the same time it is necessary that job-choice tests and various movies and filmstrips dealing with occupations, with job interviews, and with successful personal relationships become an integral part of the program. The goal of this phase of the study program is to provide an introduction to the various kinds of jobs that may be available in the community, and to provide a critical look at their own abilities and disabilities as they relate to the demands of the various kinds of jobs which might be available.

VOCATIONAL INFORMATION DURING JOB TRYOUT (Vocational Adjustment)

During this phase of the program, the vocational information course should be devoted to such things as problems having to do with union membership; group and individual insurance programs; the nature and provisions of social security; the tax system including federal income tax legal requirements, time of filing, the necessity for saving check stubs, the use of W-2 forms, the claiming of dependents, and the problems of withholding pay. In addition the student should have the opportunity to learn about the ways businesses operate, the use of warning and safety signs, the kinds of company rules which apply to specific businesses, the use of bulletin boards for employee information, as well as other more general company rules and practices.

Materials for these activities can be obtained from the Social Security Administration, from the Bureau of Internal Revenue, from the Employment Service, and directly from the bulletin boards and company manuals which are available from most large companies in many communities. In the event that a school is located in a community in which there is a paucity of industrial plants, it is desirable to visit nearby communities and obtain these materials from the plants located there. In any case all of the materials used in the Vocational Information Phase of the program should be directly related to the requirements of the job and allow the student to assess his own abilities in relationship to the requirements of the jobs being studied. It is possible that actual practice in job interviews using either an employment officer, role playing, or a visiting personnel director from industry, could become a most meaningful part of the program.

VOCATIONAL INFORMATION
DURING PERMANENT PLACEMENT

During the placement phase of the program, the study parts should involve the specific problems related to the jobs the students hold. It is recommended that these be discussed at least once a week during an evening class with the instructor or the job supervisor in charge of the program. Problems having to do with role playing in terms of social behavior and job behavior should be the core of the program. In many instances the individuals may have specific problems of reading or arithmetic which need to be attended to on a tutorial basis. In the case of remedial work in arithmetic and reading it has worked reasonably well to provide homework for the students so they may have an opportunity to work on particular knotty problems and then bring them to the class for correction and discussion. It is also recommended that at this time criticisms from employers be presented to the students so they may have a chance to discuss these criticisms and offer possible solutions to their classmates who are having problems in their job adjustment.

Perhaps of most critical importance is the discussion of problems which are directly related to independent living or to interfamily relationships. These need a thorough airing during the final phase of the program so that when the student graduates, he is not only employed but has had a trial period of employment and a thorough discussion of problems of independent living under the supervision and direction of the school personnel.

Academic subjects[2]

Two levels of academic work should be involved in the study aspects of the program. The first level is remedial or developmental work. In this the students are given the opportunity to develop their basic academic skills in reading, writing, arithmetic, and spelling to the highest possible level. Although a variety of techniques may be used to teach this developmental or remedial program, the degree to which any school may offer services may depend to a large extent on the availability of experts who help in the program. If the school should have a reading clinic as a part of its general services to students, personnel in this clinic can help the teacher develop appropriate kinds of remedial programs for specific students based on an adequate diagnosis. In the absence of such experts, the teacher may wish to develop his own remedial program. In this latter instance it is strongly recommended that extensive use be made of the literature on the teaching of academic subjects. A study by Frey and Rainey[3] indicates that teaching-machine materials are appropriate for use with mentally subnormal students and that they are highly useful to the students.

Two aspects of teaching-machine instruction seem to be critical. First of all, the machine does not represent the same kind of "authority figure" to many students that a teacher or a remedial expert represents. Therefore, students who would ordinarily be antagonistic toward any authority figure in the school tend to respond to the machine as an interesting object and not something that represents an authority to be rebelled against. Their performance, therefore, is often superior on the machines to that obtained with a teacher in charge. A second aspect is that the machines are programmed in sequential steps and mastery is assured at each step before proceeding to the next. This mastery of each step seems to be more critical for mentally subnormal youngsters than for others. Perhaps a third or corollary aspect of this sequential programming is that if the student should forget his lessons, the machine is always available for the review of critical aspects of the program. Perhaps an even more important dividend from machine instruction is that it can be done independently by the student without much supervision from the teacher. This frees the teacher to work on the other parts of the program and to concentrate on the groups of students who are in need of a study program which provides the integration of vocational and academic information.

The second level of the academic work of the work study program involves the use of materials from the jobs for academic development. This part of the program is designed to insure that the students will be able to read and understand the kinds of academic materials used in actual job performance. For this reason, all of the materials used in the practical aspects of the program should come directly from jobs or be related to jobs with which the students are familiar. These materials should then be used in an attempt to provide the necessary learnings or skills which will enable students to perform satisfactorily on the job or to read the instructions with understanding. In other words, this entire program is aimed at the practical aspects of integrating work factors in the study program.

PREVOCATIONAL ARITHMETIC

In prevocational study, arithmetic should be used to provide the basic skills and information which are related to jobs that the students are working on either in the sheltered work situations, on the work samples, or in the jobs in the school itself. Following are some suggestions which can be followed in the development of this practical arithmetic program.[4]

OUTLINE OF ARITHMETIC FOR THE BEGINNING WORKER

1. In what ways is arithmetic used on different jobs which I could do?
   A] stockboy
   B] curb service work
   C] car wash
   D] babysitting
   E] piece work

2. How much money can I make on various jobs?
    A] stockboy
    B] curb service work
    C] car wash
    D] babysitting
    E] piece work
3. What should I know before I take a job?
    A] hours of work
    B] vacation days
    C] sick leave
    D] rate of pay
    E] transportation
    F] how much money can I expect on payday
4. What should I do with my money?
    A] clothing, food, rent
    B] transportation
    C] entertainment
    D] savings accounts
    E] others
5. How can I make my money last until next payday?
    A] planning ahead with budget
    B] weekly expenses
    C] monthly expenses
    D] completed budget
6. Review of arithmetic
    A] using arithmetic on different jobs
    B] using arithmetic to gain information before starting on a job
    C] what should my paycheck come out to
    D] where the money goes
    E] keeping track of expenses

EXAMPLE OF ARITHMETIC FOR THE BEGINNING WORKER

An example of the kind of work which can be done in arithmetic is illustrated by the following story exercise. It shows "In what ways is arithmetic used on different jobs which I could do?" and is an example of piece work.

What is piece work? Suppose that someone tells you that he will pay you 5¢ for every bag of marbles that you fill. You could say that you were paid "by the bag," or to put it another way, you could say that you were paid "by the piece." This is piece work. It is used in many jobs in which packaging and packing are done.

Here are some problems using the idea of piece work. Work as many as you can.

John was hired to sort soft-drink bottles and put them into a carton. Each carton held 6 bottles. If John did 10 cartons the first hour, how many bottles did he sort?
Answer: _____

If John filled 10 cartons an hour for 4 hours, how many cartons did he fill?   Answer: _____

If each carton held 6 bottles, how many bottles did John sort in 4 hours?   Answer: _____

Susan was hired to pack beanies into cartons: each carton held 100 beanies. Susan found that she could pack 50 beanies in an hour. How long would it take her to fill the carton?   Answer: _____

If Susan worked for 4 hours, how many cartons could she fill?   Answer: _____

Obviously, questions and problems of a similar nature could be worked out to use situations encountered on the job as the basis of the arithmetic portion of the study program. It is important that as much of the study program as possible be intimately tied to the jobs with which the students are becoming familiar.

ARITHMETIC FOR THE JOB TRYOUT PHASE

At the level of vocational adjustment or job tryout, the following outline may be useful in relating arithmetic to the job.

1. Arithmetic and the job
    a) Specific job problems

2. Math and the paycheck
   a) Overtime pay
      (1) Time and a half
      (2) Double time
   b) Commissions on sales
   c) Deductions
      (1) Federal income tax
      (2) Social Security
      (3) Others
3. Arithmetic and the home
   a) Food, clothing, shelter
   b) Transportation
      (1) Initial cost of an automobile
      (2) License cost
      (3) Insurance
      (4) Financing
      (5) Tires, gasoline, oil
      (6) Repairs
   c) Checking accounts
   d) Saving Accounts
   e) Costs you never think about
   f) Personal property and real estate tax
4. Insurance
   a) Life
   b) Health
   c) Retirement

During permanent placement, specific problems arising from the job, such as those dealing with unions, insurance, and arithmetic to improve the performance of the individual on the job, should be dealt with in an individual manner. Once again the teacher will probably have to develop the materials which are needed by a specific student to solve a specific problem. This probably should be done in consultation with the employer so that a meaningful kind of activity for the student can result in better job performance.

In language arts the study program should follow the same

outline as the other academic subjects: namely, the pre-vocational, vocational adjustment or job tryout, and placement. A suggested practical application of the language arts program follows.

PREVOCATIONAL LANGUAGE ARTS

OUTLINE OF READING AND WRITING
FOR THE BEGINNING WORKER

1. In what ways are reading and writing being used on different jobs that I can do?
   a) stock boy
   b) curb service work
   c) babysitting
   d) car wash
   e) piece work
2. How can I find jobs?
   a) newspapers—in the classified advertising section
   b) signs and posters in store windows
   c) friends and relatives
   d) employment office
3. How do I apply for a job?
   a) reply to an advertisement
   b) fill out job application forms
   c) prepare for the job interview
   d) the job interview itself
4. Before I get the job?
   a) social security—What is it, and what I must do?
   b) dependents—How many am I allowed to claim?

EXAMPLE OF READING AND WRITING FOR
THE BEGINNING WORKER

A suggested activity is the development of stories which apply to various divisions of the above outline. An example of "How Do I Apply for a Job?" is shown in the following story of the job interview.

There are many things to learn about a job interview. The following story is an example of one interview. Read the story carefully and be thinking of how you might have done as well or better than John.

JOHN GETS A JOB

John was nervous; he answered an ad in the newspaper asking for a stock boy at the A & P Store. The manager, Mr. Green, called on the phone and asked John to come in for an interview. Dick and Larry, John's friends, were as excited as John.

"Now be sure to be on time," said Larry. "I will," said John. "Hey, you guys, it's getting late," said Dick. "Do I look all right?" asked John. "Sure you look fine," said Larry.

The three boys left for the store in good time. John left his friends outside and walked into the store about three minutes before the time set for the interview. He walked to the manager's office and asked for Mr. Green, the manager. The man looked up from his work and said, "I'm Mr. Green; you must be John Jones." "Yes, sir," replied John. "Come in and sit down," said Mr. Green, firmly shaking John's hand. "Thank you," said John, sitting down. "Have you ever done stock work before?" asked Mr. Green. "No, sir, but I know some of you stock boys and from the talks I have had I think I can learn to do the work," replied John. "I am very glad to hear that, John, because when I mentioned your name to your friends, they recommended you for the job," said Mr. Green. "If you decide to try me on the job, what hours would you like for me to work, Mr. Green?" asked John. "Well, after school and on Saturdays now, but probably full time in the summer," replied Mr. Green. "That would suit me just fine," said John. "Of course, we would put you on a trial period for six weeks, John; and if you do a good job and show an interest in the work, you can expect a small raise after that," said Mr. Green. "How much do you pay beginning stock boys?" said John. "Seventy-five cents an hour to start, and eighty-five cents after the trial period," replied Mr. Green. "That's a good wage," said John. "If you would like to start work on Tuesday, John, be here at 4:30 P.M., wearing a white shirt," said Mr. Green. "I'll be here," said John.

John thanked Mr. Green and hurried outside to tell the good news to his friends Dick and Larry.

EXERCISES: Go back through the story and underline any words that you had trouble understanding. Look these words up in the dictionary. Be ready to discuss the story in class. To help you, here are some questions you should answer before coming to class.
List the most important things that John did that helped him get the job.

1.

2.

3.

4.

List things that John did *not* do but which might have helped him to get the job.

1.

2.

3.

4.

LANGUAGE ARTS DURING JOB TRYOUT

During the vocational adjustment, or job tryout phase, many aspects of the job can be used for preparing stories or written materials for the language arts.

READING AND WRITING AND THE JOB

1. What are all these forms for?
   a) Social Security
   b) Federal income tax

      (1) dependents claimed
      (2) amount taken out
      (3) check stubs
      (4) W–2 forms
      (5) time of filing
      (6) legal requirements
   c) Group health insurance
      (1) advantages
      (2) disadvantages
   d) Unions
      (1) advantages
      (2) disadvantages

READING AND WRITING IN THE HOME

1. What can I find in other sections of the newspaper?
   a) different sections of the paper other than wanted ads
   b) money saved by reading the newspaper regularly (sales, classified ads, and advertisements)
2. What's in magazines?
   a) different types of magazines
3. How many different kinds of letters are there?
   a) business letters
   b) letters to friends and relatives
4. What do I have to read in order to keep my job?
   a) warning and safety signs
   b) company rules
   c) bulletin boards
   d) directions for operating machines
5. Review
   a) reading and writing on different jobs
   b) locating the jobs
   c) getting ready for the job
   d) apply for the job
   e) reading to keep the job

LANGUAGE ARTS DURING PERMANENT PLACEMENT

In the placement phase, reading and language arts should encompass those specific problems which arise on the job. These may have to do with union membership, reading, writing, and recording as they apply to a specific job or individual help with income tax, social security, and other types of forms, including withholding tax. In all instances the specific problems should be related to the job, and they should come from the students who are working on specific jobs. These can become an integral part of an evening program for discussion by the entire group.

While primary attention is being directed to practical applications of the academic subjects, the demonstrated importance of a pleasing appearance and attitude as factors in employment success demands that good health, personal grooming, and family relationships not be neglected.

The hygiene study in this sequence should be devoted primarily to the development of habits of personal grooming and good health. This should include the development of regular habits, personal cleanliness, and proper care of the body in grooming and proper diet. In order to carry on this instruction properly, it is necessary to have a wash basin and water and a triple mirror within easy accessibility of the students. Under some conditions it may be necessary to take the students to the gymnasium locker rooms to demonstrate proper methods of care. Certainly demonstrations on washing and fixing hair and the use of curlers, hair driers, bleaches, and other paraphernalia should be included. While it may be necessary to separate the boys and girls for certain kinds of activities, under most circumstances it is important that they be kept together. It has been found by many teachers that the desire to appear in a good light to the members of the opposite sex is excellent motivation for paying attention to personal habits.

An important measure in maintaining good health is diet

control, and instruction on proper diet should cover the importance of basic foods in the dairy, meat, fruit, vegetable, cereal groups, and an elementary discussion of the function of minerals, vitamins, proteins, carbohydrates, and fats in the maintenance of good health.

Both the boys and girls should be introduced to the knowledge of home economics. This should include simple cooking, clothing repair and care, diet control, and home management. Perhaps the most important aspect of this area of study involves kitchen and personal cleanliness. This vital information has often been neglected because teachers have not properly understood the need for these skills and knowledges. Yet the difference between dependent and independent living often is reflected by the degree to which one is able to maintain an apartment or light-housekeeping room, prepare his own meals and lunches in a relatively sanitary fashion, and care for his own clothing and laundry.

The opportunity to prepare and serve simple and inexpensive meals, to wash dishes, and to clean up the kitchen efficiently should be specifically provided as a part of the classroom work for both boys and girls. In addition, the students should be taught to use automatic washers for washing clothes and should learn how to iron not only flat pieces but also blouses, shirts, trousers, and skirts. These experiences need to be planned for and provided as a part of the program for teaching the skills of home management. Their importance cannot be overestimated.

Personal grooming for both boys and girls should receive the same deliberate attention and practice. Hair washing and styling, clothing selection and wear, and clothing alteration and repair should be taught to, and practiced by, both sexes. This is important to the development of skills necessary to independent living. Under some circumstances it may even be necessary to provide lockers with clean clothes so the youngsters can change clothes in school and thus learn to be conscious of cleanliness.

Studies by Cowan and Goldman[5] and by Neff[6] have pointed to the critical importance of family support in the successful employment experiences of the mentally subnormal. Unfortunately, no very clear picture of exactly what is meant by "support" emerges from the studies. While the usual meaning of "encouragement and aid" are generally accepted as important, it seems equally probable that the complete neglect or even abuse can be viewed as a kind of encouragement to get and to keep a job. That is, when a young person must work or starve, he may actually be more highly motivated to work effectively than if he knows he will be taken care of by his family. Perhaps the key concept is that of independence versus dependence. Translated into these terms, good family support could be defined as any attitudes or actions which encourage the youngster to be independent. Undesirable family support would be those attitudes or actions which foster dependence.

With this in mind, school personnel can then work with parents to encourage them to provide experiences for their children which give practice in independence: decisions, responsibilities, and activities of both a personal and a family nature.

The interpretation of the abilities and disabilities of each boy and girl to the parents is a school responsibility. Whether it is done by the teacher, work supervisor, counselor, or social worker may not be of critical importance. However, it is important that the same person do the parent counseling for any given student.

This counseling should involve a discussion of the student's progress in all of the areas: intellectual or academic, personal, social, and vocational. A most useful device has been to center the discussions about the weekly progress report and production record of the student. This can be tied to suggestions for activities which the family can provide which will be supportive of the school program. Since the students will progress through a three-phase program of prevocational, job tryout, and placement, the parents need to be kept fully informed as to the experiences being emphasized and therefore be able to adjust their activities in keeping with the school program. Co-operation between the school and the home is a most important matter.

The teacher should be careful to confine his comments to facts and avoid opinions, criticisms, and value judgments. This is a major argument for the use of production reports as a basis for discussion with parents. It also gives the teacher a sound base from which he can make suggestions to the parents to effect the improvement of performance. Perhaps a note of caution is in order: If there is one error which should be avoided, it is that of being a "teacher" to the parents. The tendency to "instruct" at the expense of listening and respecting the need for the parents to talk is a common but unnecessary error. Parents have been acquainted with their own children for a much longer time and under a greater variety of conditions than teachers. Their observations and judgments need to be heard, understood, and evaluated.

It should be kept in mind that the student will be in the program for from four to eight years. Much good can be accomplished when parents and the school officials join their efforts for this long period of time. Patience, in this instance, is a virtue well worth courting.

6

THE SHELTERED WORKSHOP

SCHOOLS have used a variety of ways of providing initial work experience for students in work study programs. It has been pointed out that one is the assignment of students to work stations within the school such as: the school cafeteria, working with the maintenance personnel, doing messenger work, or helping with clerical duties. A second method has been that of assigning the students to work stations within the business community in an attempt to bring them in contact with real-life situations early in their school careers. A third system of providing this experience has been through the use of work samples from industry. Fourth, some schools have participated in the operation of sheltered workshops.[1]

In some instances schools set up the sheltered work program and have operated their own workshop as exemplified by the Kent County, Michigan program.[2] In this program the County Special Education organization has established and operates a subcontract program. Students spend one-half day in the workshop and the other half day in the study program, thus getting a balance between work and study. They perform a variety of work tasks such as simple assembly, reclamation in the refinishing of furniture and rebuilding desks, and they have a primary manufacturing unit in which they make polyethelene raincoats for commercial sale, although on a subcontract basis.

Legislation in some states such as California now make it possible for schools to make arrangements and pay for services from already established sheltered workshops. Under this law it is possible for students to spend part of their school time in the workshops for their experience and devote the rest of their time to study geared to vocational information and academic subjects which are vocationally oriented.

The step from purchasing services from a workshop to the actual operation of a sheltered workshop or a sheltered work training program under the direction of school personnel is a short one. It is quite probable that within the foreseeable future many more schools will start their own sheltered workshops or work training programs using actual work on subcontract, reclamation, and perhaps manufactured materials.

A sheltered workshop is an anomaly in this western culture. In a world of business, industrial and social competition where merit as measured by accomplishment is a guiding principle of operation, the sheltered workshop stands as a contradiction. It is not self-supporting. It is not competitive. Its administrative and supervisory personnel are clinically trained, and are service, rather than profit, oriented. Most unusual is that whereas industry employs workers to make or assemble a product, the sheltered workshop employs a product to produce workers. This frankly places the workshop in the role of a teaching institution; yet the workshop is viewed by many as a business venture.

Two opposing economic positions are pertinent to this discussion.[3] Both are aimed at increasing the gross national product; yet they approach this goal from opposite directions. Briefly (and perhaps oversimplified) one philosophy holds that vocationally handicapped people should be trained to enter the labor market on a competitive basis and be rewarded and judged on the basis of their accomplishments as is any other worker. Concessions should be neither given nor asked for and if the handicapped person cannot compete, he should join the welfare rolls to be cared for by a benevolent arm of society—the local, state or federal government. His contribution will be either through his production, or the spending of his welfare checks. In either case, he does not interfere with the competitive requirements of the system since his work role is the same as any nonhandicapped worker. Taxation returns are earmarked for his training or care and are administered from outside the competitive system by governmental agencies which are supported by, but outside the workings of the system. The results of rehabilitative efforts are judged by the relationship of the earnings of the handicapped worker before rehabilitation, the cost of his rehabilitation and his earnings after rehabilitation. Quite often these costs are compared with some formula estimates of welfare or institutional costs. But the test is the amount of the contribution over and above the rehabilitation cost.

The opposition position supports and allows for the planned contribution of the handicapped workers in a governmentally operated or subsidized shop. A portion of the economic product is earmarked for the exclusive use of the shop. The difference between the production cost of the product and its economic return to the shop is frankly subsidized by the governmental agency as a cost of caring for the disabled. Such an arrangement is quite common in many European countries such as England, Holland and the Scandinavian countries. In Holland, for example, the institutionalized disabled may work as farm labor on a contractual basis during the summers and harvest. During the winter and in inclement weather they are employed in such industrial pursuits as a factory which makes paper boxes. This is a governmentally subsidized business which can exist because of the subsidy and in spite of the inefficiency of its labor force. The welfare funds are invested in the factory operation for the support of the business which, in turn, supports the workers. A portion of the tax dollar is therefore invested in a business which lets the handicapped worker contribute whatever his talents may be to the production of a commodity which increases the gross national product.

At base, both approaches provide for a means of using the talents of the handicapped for the welfare of the economy. Both call for governmental intervention in the lives of the handicapped. Both involve tax monies for the good of the less fortunate and less well-equipped citizens. The first approach, however, keeps the government out of business. The second puts the government squarely in business through subsidy. More specifically, the first approach asks the disabled to disavow that they are handicapped, while the second allows the disabled person to be productive up to the limits of his handicap without fear of discrimination because he cannot be as productive as his nonhandicapped peers. Child labor laws protect children because they are immature. Governmental subsidy of business for the disabled can protect the disabled because they are disabled. Fundamentally, both groups are disadvantaged—unable to compete successfully with nonhandicapped adults. Yet it seems strange that while there is no reluctance among governmental legislative bodies to pass laws which protect children or which subsidize farmers, they have not expressed their concern for the disabled by subsidizing workshops on a continuing basis.

The current practice of partial and limited federal support under the "seed-money" concept seems to be a good beginning. That is, money for demonstration or research projects which use sheltered workshops for the training of the handicapped is extensive, both quantitatively and geographically. These funds, however, are typically granted in decreasing amounts for from one to three years with the expectation that local funds will be found to replace the original federal subsidy. That this does happen has been demonstrated repeatedly in widely differing and geographically separated programs. Yet those programs which have survived have done so through the valiant efforts of dedicated staff and boards of directors. Typically, they have found supporting funds from a wealthy benefactor, from community or United Funds, from a private organization or several organizations, from churches or other religious groups, from service clubs, from tuitions of clients in training under the sponsorship of Divisions of Vocational Rehabilitation, from subcontract, reclamation or manufacturing profits or from some combination of these.

Persisting laments from staff and boards of directors attest to the difficulties and potential, if not real, abuses which grow out of such financial problems. The financial problems become so great that the rehabilitative welfare of the clients can become of secondary importance to the financial survival of the program. Thus clients on tuition may be preferred to non-tuition clients. Tuition extensions may almost automatically be requested. Efficiency experts may be employed to devise more efficient production procedures. Productive workers may be kept in the shops while their less capable companions are dropped from the rolls. Specific additional research or demonstration grants may be solicited which make it possible to support staff members who double in brass by functioning in both the new and the older parts of the program. In short, the handicapped may be exploited— paid less than they should and production rather than training becomes the goal. To many professionals in this field the need for services and the benefits which accrue to the clients from even a marginal program are so great that they are willing to undergo almost any personal hardship including sharp twinges of conscience to preserve the programs. Yet how much better these programs would be if the staff could devote its energies to rehabilitation rather than economic survival activities. A continuing support base could assure this wise use of staff energies to rehabilitation rather than economic survival activities thus increasing many fold the utility and worth of the workshop programs to the disabled.

To accomplish the goal of continuing governmental subsidy of workshops, a fundamental reorientation in the philosophy of rehabilitation may be required. New and basic legislation, certainly is required. (Recent federal legislation in the war on poverty is a step in that direction.) Until this is done, programs for the mentally subnormal in the public school can contribute to the stability of the workshop. By furnishing a continuing supply of tuition-paying students from the school to already existing workshops, a guaranteed income for the workshop can be assured. The alternative of a school-sponsored workshop also assures continuing support of the services and allows the professional staff to concentrate on the needs of the handicapped worker rather than on the problem of economic survival. In any case, it seems most important to the welfare of handicapped students, that schools make fuller use of existing workshop services than they have in the past.

While it is possible that the schools may be able to purchase services from already existing sheltered workshops, in many instances it is necessary and perhaps desirable for the school personnel to operate their own sheltered work training program. There are many advantages to the latter operation. First, it is possible for the school personnel to select the kind of work which will be most meaningful and give the largest variety of experiences to their students. Second, since the schools already have an existing administrative framework for record keeping, purchasing, administration, and supervision, it is probable that public schools can start a sheltered work training program at less cost than an independent organization (which would have to develop its own bookkeeping and record keeping, purchasing system, supervisory and administrative personnel). Third, it seems likely that a greater articulation between the students' activities in the work program and the study program could be effected if the school has the supervision and the control of both aspects of this training. If a school system elects to use a sheltered workshop, either school or community operated, certain evaluations need to be made concerning its functions. The following sections are presented to give a basic picture of sheltered workshop programs.[4]

Organization of the sheltered workshop
Purposes

The purpose of any work training program should be to evaluate the potential and identify the vocational objectives of handicapped students and to provide vocational experience in a controlled environment. This should operate in two ways. First, the work center should serve as an evaluation and training facility to provide definitive evaluation of the students' potential for employability and to assist the student in developing the skills and attitudes to increase this potential. For most students this would be a relatively short program, perhaps a year, with the expectation that they would then be moved into job tryout, or vocational adjustment, and then into permanent employment. Another advantage of maintaining a work training center is the possibility of increasing, if necessary, the time which a student could spend in that aspect of the program thus giving him a longer period of time in which to increase his vocational skills prior to the time that he is placed on job tryout.

A second purpose of the program is that of permanent placement for some of the less skilled students. It is quite possible that some of these individuals may have to be in a protected kind of environment for the better part of their lives; therefore, this facility could provide for the long-term placement of these less skilled individuals.

Facilities required

While some school systems have a suitable kind of facility for the location of this type of program, it is probable that many school systems would have to look for a suitable building away from the local school environment. In choosing such a location school officials should be sure that the building complies with all city fire and safety regulations. It should have adequate light, ventilation, and facilities for heating and cooling. It must have adequate washroom facilities for both ambulatory and non-ambulatory students. Of critical importance is the necessity for having adequate facilities for storage, for shipping of the finished products, and for receiving of the raw materials. Before storage facilities are considered adequate it must be determined that walls and foundations of the building are suitable to sustain the weight of the finished products, raw materials and machinery involved. It should be located in such a place that public transportation is available and can be used by the students to get to and from the work center itself.

Although the requirements for space would vary greatly according to the work done and the number of students in the program, certain standard requirements have been established by workshop and work training center personnel. It has generally been accepted that in an operation of subcontract, reclamation, and manufacturing work a minimum of one-hundred square feet per student must be allowed. For an operation to serve fifty students, for example, and to include locker, washroom, and lunchroom facilities as well as office and reception room space, shipping and receiving facilities, storage for raw and for completed goods as well as actual work space, an absolute minimum of five-thousand square feet must be provided. Obviously, if the nature of the work is only subcontract work of a light assembly or reclamation nature, the space requirements would not be so great. It would be desirable, however, to plan for additional storage and workshop space required for new operations and for the possibility of expanding into manufacturing work. Obviously, the existence of assembly-line type of operation would also make it possible to have somewhat smaller space requirements than where work stations are set up for each individual.

Equipment

Equipment required also varies with the type of work to be done, but certain equipment is basic. Office equipment such as desks, chairs, file cabinets, typewriters, adding machine, mimeograph machine, reception and lounge furniture, and a tape recorder would be considered minimum.

In the shop area, work tables of sit-down and stand-up height, must be provided along with adjustable metal chairs. An assortment of hand tools and such miscellaneous items as fire extinguishers, dollies, hand truck, time clock with card rack, fans, and scales are basic regardless of the work performed. Basic beginning power tools would probably include a drill press, a jigsaw, table saw, electric handsaw, belt sander, and at least two sewing machines. Additions to these basic equipment items would depend on the type of work to be done and perhaps would include such things as heat sealers, routers, jointers, or other special tools which are required to do the work of the contracts.

It is generally more convenient if a basic lunchroom facility can be provided. This does not necessarily mean the serving of hot meals, but it should contain a refrigerator, storage cupboard, tables, chairs, coffee pots and the opportunity for the students to eat their lunches in a more or less industrial setting.

One very important item to be considered with equipment is a means of transportation. This might be a heavy-duty stationwagon or carry-all or light truck. Subcontract work can be arranged for much more successfully if there is a pickup and delivery on small items. There must also be a means of securing supplies for the workshop as well as transportation in contacting potential clients and making contacts for possible subcontract work.

Personnel

For the successful operation of a work training center, the personnel will vary with the nature of the handicaps of the students enrolled and the type and extent of the program. At a very minimum, however, the personnel should consist of a director, a workshop supervisor, and a secretary-book-keeper. This amount of staff will allow for a maximum of twenty students. If the work center is to grow, however, the director must be free to contact potential subcontract businesses and to seek markets for goods which may be manufactured. Since much of the director's work would take him away from the workshop, twenty students is a maximum that can be supervised by one supervisor. Even serving this many students is possible only if the group has both physically handicapped and mentally handicapped students. This makes it possible to utilize the abilities of the physically handicapped students to help in the decision making which the mentally retarded students may not be able to make. Under come circumstances it may be possible to use college students, particularly those in the area of special education, guidance, or other fields of rehabilitation as part-time assistants, or under some circumstances it might be possible to arrange for volunteer help from the community itself. It should be noted, however, that in the case of community volunteers it is necessary to provide careful and continuing supervision for their work and to assure that the necessary volunteers are at the workshop at specified times.

DIRECTOR

As a general rule the director should have the responsibility for the establishment of work center policies and standards. He should have the responsibility for recruitment of both professional and clerical staff and should provide for their orientation and instruction in their respective jobs. He should also be the sole individual responsible for the dismissal of personnel under established procedures. A major portion of his job would be to make contact with business associations and unions, locate, and obtain the use of various industrial directories, arrange for telephone and mail solicitations, visit local industrial plants, arrange for the smooth flow of clients from the work center to job tryouts and vocational adjustment, and solicit subcontracts and reclamation work for the work center.

In addition, he would have the responsibility for developing marketable items for production, for gathering the necessary information concerning costs and sources of raw materials, and for determining the necessary procedures for marketing. He should also be responsible for formulating evaluation and training programs designed to provide a program for the evaluation of the potential of the workshop students. Particularly in the early development of the workshop, he has the responsibility for maintaining records of student progress and for calling staff meetings in which the students are discussed and planned for in terms of increasing their potential. Last, but far from least, he would be responsible for representing the workshop before interested individuals and organizations, both lay and professional, to present a consistent picture of the program and the service of the work training center.

WORKSHOP SUPERVISOR

The workshop supervisor should be responsible for making and keeping commitments for production schedules, the quality of products manufactured under the subcontracts, and the adherence to manufacturing specifications. He should be involved in the negotiations of prices on subcontracts and have the primary responsibility for the contractors' materials. Under his jurisdiction would be shop relations with customers, including any complaints, doing time studies for price-setting purposes, and determining the operational procedure in setting up new lines of work.

A part of his responsibility would be to arrange work stations to provide the maximum variation in working conditions so that observation and evaluation may be made of each student's ability to function under a wide variety of conditions of work and supervision. He would work under the direction of the director and be responsible to him for the workshop operation. In addition, he would be responsible for the supervision of the students, the maintenance of records of attendance, of production, and of student progress. His would be the responsibility of maintaining conditions which would be conducive to the safety of the students and to instruct and guide them in their work assignments and in their observation of the safety rules. He may also be called upon to supervise the maintenance workers, to assist in time studies for the determination of wages for the students in the work center, to organize and to plan production, and to establish quality control for work in progress. He must maintain records on receiving and shipping materials. He may be called upon to purchase materials for production, to supervise shipping, and to keep a schedule of the work production so that contracted work will be prepared in time for delivery under terms of the contracts.

SECRETARY-BOOKKEEPER

One of the jobs of critical importance is the secretary-bookkeeper. In addition to the usual clerical and general office work such as taking dictation, typing letters and reports, and filing, this individual should have a knowledge of double-entry bookkeeping, a background in cost accounting particularly that relative to a small operation and be able to compute a payroll. In addition this person should maintain the students' records including the memorandum records of reports due, the date reports are sent, a record of individual earnings, individual production, and other pertinent material for the student file. It is imperative that the secretary-bookkeeper be able to maintain cost records relative to production, including the cost of the goods, direct labor, and overhead and also be able to assist in computing costs from time studies.

Monthly inventory records on raw goods and finished goods and the responsibility for billing and for accounts receivable would be a part of this person's responsibility. At the same time it would be necessary for the secretary-bookkeeper to keep the accounts payable current and to prepare monthly balance sheets showing all workshop assets and liabilities and profits and losses for each fiscal period.

It is highly desirable that this individual be imaginative and creative enough to suggest methods of increasing the services for the student and at the same time finding more efficient methods for cutting down on the cost of workshop operation. Such a service is impossible to overestimate in terms of its importance to the entire operation.

Curriculum

Since the chief function of the work center is to provide for an accurate evaluation of the employment potential of the student and to give him experience in a variety of different work and supervisor conditions, the curriculum of the workshop should be planned specifically to provide for these functions. Experiences should be planned to progress through a graded series of job levels. The jobs should be graded from those which are the simplest to those which are the most complex and from those which require little or no supervision to those which require almost constant supervision. Production standards should be set for each level for purposes of determining the student's progress. The student's readiness to move to the next higher job level should be determined by his meeting production standards at each preceding level. If he fails to meet the production standard for any level, he should be retained at that level until he does meet those standards.

Work to be sought for the center will probably be light industrial in nature. But an attempt should be made to provide a range of jobs from those which are completely unskilled to a fairly high level of semiskilled operation. In addition, it may be necessary to make arrangements for the manufacture and sale of one or more items in order to provide a steady backlog of work and offer the variety in the various stages of manufacturing which are necessary for the evaluation and training of the students.

One of the critical aspects of this program should be that of pay for the students. The rate of pay should be on a piece work basis at a level comparable to what workers would receive if they were doing the job in industry. Although the students may produce only one item per hour, whereas the norm for the industry may be ten per hour, they would be paid as nearly as possible the same amount per item as the worker in industry. This aspect of the operation assumes great proportions both for the motivation of the client and for providing a realistic situation in the academic or the study area of the program through the computation of pay, withholding tax, and production records. The entire program should stress not the specific skills which are required to work at a particular job but rather the work habits that any employee, however skilled, needs for successful employment. These include punctuality, dependability, desirable personal habits, co-operation with supervisors and other students, safety consciousness, care of materials and property, initiative, fatigue tolerance, type of routine accepted, type of supervision accepted, and the ability to work under pressure.

Type of work

Subcontract work will naturally be dependent upon the kinds of industries which are immediately available within the community in which the work center is located.[5] Such work as the assembly of play and tool kits, simple games, packaging of materials, and the assembly of simple light industrial items, have been used successfully in many parts of the country. Perhaps one of the most unique operations is located in Lincoln, Nebraska and is under the auspices of Goodwill Industries. In addition to the manufacturing and subcontracting center, this program also operates a farm and engages in the production and sale of eggs; the repair, maintenance, and assembly of farm machinery; the production of stock including cattle, swine, and sheep; and the raising of grain and feed crops. This is an excellent example of adapting the work training to the needs which are evident in the locality.

While the subcontract work has generally been thought of as the most typical kind of work in the work centers, many work center personnel have found it necessary to engage in primary manufacturing of some simple items. A work center in Louisiana, for example, manufactures caskets for pets. Another in South Dakota manufactures wooden cases for carrying milk cartons. The Employment Training Center at Southern Illinois University makes and sells "beanies" for college freshmen. In most instances the workshop personnel have engaged in this kind of operation in order to smooth out the fluctuation in the supply of subcontracts available. When the subcontracts are plentiful, the manufactured items are cut back in production. When the subcontracts begin to fall off, then the work slack is taken up by the manufactured item. In essence this becomes a stabilizing factor in the work experience load which is available for the evaluation and training of the students in the workshop.

Reclamation of a variety of items has also followed local trends. One of the more common of the reclamation projects has been that of the repair of soft drink cases. This is done in a number of workshops in many different parts of the country. Another has been the reclamation of paper which is baled and then sold to paper companies. In many instances industries will have jobs which they consider to be nuisance work.[6] An alert work center director can ask the plant personnel for this kind of work which can then be used in the training of the students and can be moved out of the parent plant to the obvious benefit of both parties.

Operating costs

It should be clearly understood that this type of facility probably never will be self-supporting. The profits from sub-contracts, reclamation, or manufacturing should not be counted upon to provide for the operating cost with the possible exception of some overhead costs. Donations to the workshop in the form of equipment or space can cut considerably the initial cost of organization. If volunteer labor is available, this can be useful as can college students for supervisory purposes on a part-time basis.

Contracts and reclamation work can provide only a very small amount for overhead. As was stated, it is important that the pay on the contracts should nearly cover what a normal worker would receive per item if he were going to do this work in industry. Obviously, any businessman who lets a sub-contract, is not going to pay the workshop more to do the work than he would pay to have it done in his own place of business. Furthermore, if the work is unusually profitable, he is not going to subcontract it at all. Thus most of the money received from subcontracts will be paid out in wages.

A somewhat higher profit can be realized from the manufacture of new goods since all of the profit from this will return to the workshop. However, an analysis of the production rate to be expected in relation to the amount of supervisory staff required, will show that this type of work will not earn a great deal of money either. Furthermore the cost of marketing may be prohibitive.

The safest method to figure the costs for operating is to assume that no monetary returns to the workshop from either contracts or manufacturing could be used for operation at least to begin with. This will mean that there should be money on hand for the rental of space, for the purchase of initial equipment, for local travel expenses, and for staff salaries. In addition, there should be available a revolving fund for the purchase of contract supplies. The exact amount for each of these categories is difficult to estimate. Nevertheless, the revolving funds should be roughly equivalent to the accounts receivable of the workshop at any one time. A very rough estimate of the first year's total expense is that it might be as high as $40,000 for the total operation. This is based on an estimate of approximately $15,000 to $18,000 for salaries, equipment costs in the neighborhood of $10,000 to $15,000, rental and utilities around $3,000 and a revolving fund of from $3,000 to $5,000. While it is possible that any of these costs may be reduced somewhat through donations or gifts from the community, it is probable that a cost analysis will show that somewhere near the $40,000 figure will have to be in cash or in equivalent donation of space, time, equipment, or materials. Perhaps the worst mistake that any agency can make in the estimate of its cost is to fail to recognize donations or gifts in terms of their true monetary value. By counting only the actual cash outlay costs, it is possible to get a grossly underestimated view of the actual cost of such an operation.

Services available to the sheltered workshop

Although many communities can make significant contributions to the operation of a work training shop, perhaps the most significant contribution can be made through the local Division of Vocational Rehabilitation. A number of school systems have found it important to seek advice from these highly skilled vocational counselors in the initial operation of their program. The Division of Vocational Rehabilitation can furnish, under some circumstances, tuitions to help the actual costs of the workshop. Not only is this a vital service to many of the students during their early contact with their world of work, but it is important that the vocational counselor be made aware of the kinds of students and the potential which they may have for future work. His early entry into the programming and planning for the students may save him hours of work and many thousands of dollars in expenses later. It is important, therefore, that the school or agency which operates the workshop have a very close liaison with this rehabilitation agency early in the career of each student. It is strongly urged that workshop personnel include the local rehabilitation counselor in their staff conferences concerning student welfare and the discussion of the progress and potential of the students. This insures that the attention of the rehabilitation counselor will be called to those cases where he can provide services at a time most critical to the student.

Advisory committees

The advisory committees for a work training center may be of two kinds. The most common kind of advisory committee is made up of representatives of the various business, professional, labor, and service organizations in the community. It has as its chief function the determining of policy and systems of operation for the work center. To a degree this advisory committee can be used as a means of entry for the workshop personnel into the business and labor community in securing services, work experience, and work placement for the students. There is no particular objection to this kind of an advisory committee, but it should be clearly understood that the function of a committee is primarily that of guidance and public relations.

A second kind of committee can be termed a "work committee." This is a committee that supervises the operation of the work center and is made up primarily of professional personnel. This kind of advisory committee generally would include personnel such as the psychologist, social worker, work supervisor, and director of the work training center, and it would primarily be concerned with specific workshop operation, student evaluation, and programming for the individual students. Such a committee is concerned essentially with the day-by-day operation of the workshop and with the experiences which the students are getting within the work training center itself. It is not concerned with public relations as such nor with entry into the business and labor community but would have its contact with the community at large primarily through parent contacts and the solicitation of services from other service organizations as they appear to be important for the welfare and the progress of the students in the program.

Many workshops have found it important to have both kinds of committees on a permanent basis and have clearly delineated the responsibilities of the two committees so that there is no danger of overlap in function. In any case the director of the work training center should be the liaison between both committees in that he should be the executive director of each of the committees.

Records

Two types of records should be kept. The first kind of records are those that are involved with the progress of the student himself. In this instance the type of work in which the student has been involved, the length of time he has been on the job, his production record, and the relationship of that production to norms for the particular kind of work involved should be kept on a daily basis and summarized at the end of each week for pay and guidance purposes. In connection with this, a record such as the progress report shown in the Appendix can also be kept to summarize student progress over a longer period of time. By using the same type of record in the work center as that used in the other aspects of the entire secondary program, progress can be noted over the entire work-study career of the student. Furthermore, specific areas of weakness can be identified and program planning to attempt to strengthen the weak performance of the student may be based on the accurate observation of his progress.

This becomes a critical factor in the judgments which must be made as to the readiness of the student for competitive work, the type of work which he may be suited for, and the possibility that he may be able to succeed under different and varying kinds of conditions.

The second kind of records which are important are those which are concerned with the operation of the workshop itself. This includes such things as the complete double-entry records of the operation. It would also include cost accounting, payroll, memorandum records of reports due, individual earning records, individual production records, maintenance cost records relative to production (including the cost of goods), direct labor and overhead, and inventory records on both raw goods and finished goods. Such things as billings and accounts receivable and payable with balance sheets should be kept on a monthly basis. In addition, all production records should be summarized and included in the cost accounting of the entire operation. It should be emphasized that the workshop records should be compatible with the kinds of records kept in any small manufacturing or business concern. They are primarily of interest to the business end of the program and have very little to do with the student records. Nevertheless, it is extremely important that these be well, accurately, and systematically kept so that the financial condition of the workshop is always apparent to the workshop director and the advisory board.

One of the great temptations for individuals who are responsible for workshop direction is to place the business operation of the workshop ahead of the welfare of the students. Perhaps one reason why many school organizations have considered going into the workshop business is because they can control the setting for the welfare of the students rather than the business interest of the operation. This suggests that a school-operated work training program can be more legitimately run at a loss than a workshop which depends upon its support from meeting work production schedules, soliciting profitable contract work, engaging in manufactured items which show a substantial profit, soliciting tuition from rehabilitation and other service agencies and asking for other support from community and private organizations. In the school-operated training center it is possible to concentrate instead on providing a rich variety of services to the students, furnishing the necessary social workers' contacts with the student and with his home, and providing for the wholesome recreational programs as a part of the total experience of the student. Thus, although the school-operated training center is not so economically efficient as one operated by a private agency in the community, it is apt to be much more helpful to the development of the student in that it can provide a variety of experiences other than those which are primarily work experiences to aid in his overall development.

This latter fact has been cited as a source of weakness in the school-operated program by some. The argument in this case seems to run that if the student is to learn what the world of work is like, he should be exposed to as realistic a work situation as possible. If the work situation in the work training center is operated for the convenience of the student rather than with strict adherence to economic efficiency, the student gets a distorted view of what the world of work may be like and is, therefore, being robbed of a vital aspect of his training. Which may be the most valid argument would depend to a great extent on the community in which the program may be located. That is to say, the philosophies of the individuals who run the program may be of much greater importance than either the efficiency of the operation or the program supporting the work experiences in the general development of the students' employability potential. For example, if it is possible to get the supporting services and experiences through other media than the work center itself, it may be quite feasible and important to run a highly efficient industrial-like operation which is as realistic as possible in terms of its work performance demands. On the other hand, if this is the best facility, and if the personnel are available, able, and interested in providing the other supporting experiences, perhaps the efficiency of the work experience may not be so important as the other services rendered. This is largely a matter of local determination. However, it is important that the students have an opportunity for a realistic work experience either in the work center, in their job tryout, or vocational adjustment phase, of the program, or in the actual job placement. And it is perhaps equally important that they have the opportunity to develop the skills of social participation, the insights which can be achieved through both personal and vocational advisement, and the support of a family which is solidly behind the student in his attempts to develop his vocational proficiency.

Use of already existing workshops

Should the school personnel decide to use already existing work centers for the work experience of their students, certain considerations must be kept in mind. First, it is important that the students receive some remuneration from work which they do commensurate with their rate of production. This is seen as an immediate feedback mechanism which allows the students to gain insights into his own behavior from readily available information concerning his performance. If he is working at a submarginal level, this is apparent because the rate of pay is lower than that which his companions in the work center are getting. On the other hand, if he receives a rather high rate of pay, this is tangible evidence that his production is good and that he may expect to soon be given the opportunity to work in the job tryout phase of the program.

A second consideration is that of tuitions. In many instances the school officials may feel that it is not possible to pay a tuition to a workshop for the services which the students receive. An alternative is that of placing their students in the workshop on a half-pay basis. With this arrangement, half of the amount of money earned by each student would be returned to him in the form of wages and the other half would be kept by the work center to help pay for the cost of supervision and materials used to provide the experiences for the student. In any case it is important that the school officials realize that this is a legitimate kind of service for which they must pay.

A third consideration is that no student should be moved from the work center into the job tryout or vocational adjustment phase of the program until he demonstrates the vocational, personal, and social competencies judged to be important in a competitive work assignment. When this level of efficiency has been reached, the student may properly be advanced to the job tryout or vocational adjustment phase of the program.

It should be emphasized that the length of time needed by the student in any aspect of his training is secondary to the level of skill development. The goal is an employable person, not a neat administrative program package.

7

A SUMMARY

A high school work-study program for the mentally sub-normal must be based on a definitive description of their characteristics and a clear statement of the objectives to be achieved. Furthermore, it should be consistent with the social, economic, and political milieu in which these people will live.

Recorded changes in socio-political philosophies have brought increasing emphases to the humanistic values of equality and acceptance of all individuals. This points up sharply the ever-increasing need for each individual in this society to be given the opportunity to develop his abilities to the fullest.

How this may be best accomplished by individuals who have the unfortunate disability of subnormal mental development is not fully clear. The concept of what is meant by mental subnormality is one confusing factor. Although definitions are plentiful, they tend to concentrate on either the sociological, medical, educational or psychological aspects and fail to unify all of the complexities of the condition. Even the general classification system of the American Association on Mental Deficiency emphasizes only the characteristic of "inadequate mental development" as common to all individuals in this group.[1] The one common factor therefore becomes subaverage individual intelligence test performance. This is certainly an inadequate basis for a curriculum.

Although early workers in the field deduced a program from the axiological statement of Itard[2] and Seguin[3] that mental subnormality was a result of lack of sufficient and appropriate environmental stimuli during the persons' formative years, this statement has been disproved and discarded. It now appears that there is both a physiological and an environmental basis for subnormal mental development. The extent and pervasiveness of each seems to vary from individual to individual with little information available to indicate the contribution of each to the final functioning level of any given person. The monumental work of Kirk[4] is a significant beginning in this field, but it is far from definitive and has not been sufficiently extended to furnish concrete answers to the nature-nurture question.

In the absence of an axiological base for curriculum, there remains only the evidence from empirical and experiential findings. From these, it is apparent that the characteristics which contribute to the employability of the mentally subnormal are some combination of their intellectual, personal, social and vocational skills used in concert or in some yet undiscovered mutually-compensating combinations. From a purely rational point of view, it seems evident that the program must be designed to deal with a person with little aptitude or desire for learning, with limited experience and with few abilities for realistic goal setting. He must be trained in an easily understandable program of experiences which lead systematically to permanent job placement and independent living. Provision must be made for the opportunity to learn the critical skills in each of the important areas of work and living.

Such is the program described in this manuscript. It combines work and related study through three stages of experience: prevocational training through vocational information and experience in sheltered-work conditions; job tryout or vocational adjustment; supervised vocational (permanent) placement; and an adjusted academic program which is intimately co-ordinated with the vocational program.

Prevocational training should incorporate vocational information and sheltered work experience at the very start of the students' high school experience. This can be accomplished by assigning the students to jobs on the school campus, by using work samples secured from industry, or by purchasing services from an already established sheltered workshop or by establishing a school sponsored workshop. The student should be paid for his work from the start.

The recommended academic program includes making job analysis, doing personal characteristics assessment, and academic activities related to the jobs being analyzed. Problems of personal health, grooming, and social relations should receive special attention.

Integration of the students into other activities in the school should be practiced as much as possible. This should include assignment of students to various homerooms in the school, their inclusion in regular programs of physical education, shop, home economics, driver training, and other academic classes, if they are appropriate.

A systematic effort to enlist the support of parents should be integral to the program.

Work experiences in business establishments in the community is the core of the vital job tryout, or vocational adjustment, stage of the program. In effect, businessmen become adjunct instructors by providing work experience to the students on a rotating basis. The chief objective of this portion of the program is to provide a series of diverse job experiences to each student in the program. Careful and continuing supervision by school personnel is mandatory for its success. Most critical, however, is the attitude of the businessmen who offer their establishments as extensions of the school for training purposes.

The academic program should continue and extend whatever integrations of academic subjects and vocational training were begun in prevocational training. In addition, it is recommended that liberal use be made of materials from businesses to teach language arts and arithmetic. Continued attention to problems of personal conduct and appearance and home management is essential.

Perhaps the most unique part of this program is the preparation of the students for permanent job placement. This is done by providing practice first in job finding using sources such as newspapers and employment agencies. Next the students need practice in filling out various kinds of actual application blanks. They are then ready to practice job interviews; first in the classroom through role-playing and then in actual business. Their performances should be thoroughly criticized by the instructor until an acceptable level of performance is achieved.

The final phase of the program centers on performance in the world of work. The full-time performance of the student in his job situation and his living habits off the job become the primary focus. Both should be supervised by school personnel. The performance of the student is the ultimate test of the effectiveness of the other phases and experiences. The academic part of the program should be confined to evening or late afternoon classes which use for subject matter the problems encountered by the working students.

For some students additional attention will need to be given to specific reading and arithmetic skills needed for the successful performance of their jobs. Others will need help in behavior and social skills. All the activities have in common the development of individuals who are personally, socially, and vocationally independent. In this pursuit the earning of a high school diploma or certificate and participation in graduation exercises (without prejudice) should be provided.

Personnel

The very comprehensiveness of this program indicates the need for personnel who have extensive training of a kind not usually provided in many college training programs. This includes teachers, vocational supervisors, and workshop directors and supervisors.

Teachers

Since this program uses materials from the work experiences of the students in the academic part of the program, the training of teachers for this program should include provisions for learning about the academic demands of jobs typically performed by the mentally subnormal. At the bachelor's degree level, the college training program should include the usual basic courses in teacher preparation such as child and adolescent development, educational psychology, and pupil evaluation. In addition a survey of the education of exceptional children, psychological and educational problems of the mentally subnormal, methods of teaching the adolescent mentally subnormal, and practice teaching are standard requirements. Teachers of these children, however, are expected to be able to teach grooming; health habits; cooking; clothing selection, maintenance and repair; budgeting; buying; job interviewing; and home management. It is therefore highly desirable that specific units on these areas be included in the teacher preparation program. These may be offered through the school or department of home economics or they could be included as a part of the methods and materials offerings of a department of special education, but they should not be neglected. Practice teaching experience should be provided in special classes in a vocationally oriented secondary school under the supervision of an experienced master teacher. Because such secondary programs are relatively scarce, some colleges may experience difficulty in locating suitable facilities for practice teaching. An alternative, therefore, may be to use behavior training programs in already existing sheltered workshops. This is better training for teaching the mentally subnormal than is the usual practice teaching experience in an academically oriented high school program. If a college cannot locate either a vocationally oriented program in a high school or a behavior training program in a workshop setting, it may be considered the wisest course to not attempt to train secondary teachers of the mentally subnormal until suitable practice teaching facilities do become available.

Vocational supervisors

Problems of job analysis, personal, social and vocational skill evaluations, work placement and supervision, and parent contacts are the principle tasks of the vocational supervisors. Their training should provide specifically for learning these demanding skills. Basically they are teachers. Their training should include the experiences indicated as important in the preparation of teachers of secondary level special classes for the mentally subnormal. In addition, these supervisors need to learn at first hand those techniques necessary for job analysis, pupil skill evaluation, work supervision, and parent contacts. These can be taught as units in the methods and materials offerings of a department of special education in conjunction with practice teaching experiences in a special program in a high school. If no such program is available to the college personnel responsible for this training, a sheltered workshop can be utilized. In some instances, professional personnel in programs of distributive education can be of great aid since many of their techniques are quite applicable to the programs for the mentally subnormal. However, the job of the vocational supervisors is one demanding a well trained person. If a college lacks the personnel, facilities or experience to provide thorough training, it probably should not venture into this field at all.

Workshop personnel
DIRECTORS

Some school systems may wish to start their own workshops for training their students. Personnel needed to operate such facilities are in need of quite different training than teachers or vocational supervisors. The duties of workshop directors are detailed in Chapter 6. To prepare them for these duties specific programs which combine both practical experience in workshops with formal courses are being developed by many universities and colleges. While these programs differ from college to college, they have in common some critical elements. Nearly all, for example, are two year, master's degree level programs. They typically include courses in principles of accounting, industrial management, psychological and medical aspects of disabilities, principles of and practice in counseling and assessment, and evaluation techniques. The practical experiences which accompany the coursework include all phases of the workshop operation; business procedures, client selection, programming and evaluation, contract procurement, advisory committee relations, reporting and client placement and supervision. This must take place in a work center under the careful direction and supervision of college or university professional personnel.

While it may be desirable for the workshop directors to have earned teaching certificates, this is not critical. It is critical that they have practical experience in a workshop setting.

SUPERVISORS

No universal agreement concerning the training of workshop supervisors exists. Some workshops require that workshop supervisors be skilled in psychological counseling techniques. Others favor persons with supervisory experience in industry. Others prefer to employ people clinically trained in psychological or educational areas. Still others look to persons trained as social workers. These preferences are a clear reflection of the differing emphases of specific workshops. In any case, it seems important that the sponsors of the workshops be aware of what kind of environment they wish to create and employ the personnel to implement the desired emphasis. A client centered workshop would need supervisors oriented toward education, psychology, sociology or rehabilitation. A work-centered program would need persons with experience in industry. One of the most practical approaches to this problem seems to be the sponsorship of short-term training programs by colleges and universities as part of their extension services. These two- or four-week programs can have whatever emphases are dictated by the wishes of the participants.

Research needs

The practical problems of student selection, training, supervision, and placement appear so glaring and formidable that there may be a tendency to believe these to be the foremost research needs. Granted, there is an immediate urgency to systematically investigate and find answers to these pressing problems, but there remain more fundamental issues demanding attention. Hopefully, both kinds of problems could be attacked, sometimes simultaneously.

Among the most important of the practical considerations are those of determining the ingredients of a training program contributing to successful employed graduates. Basic to this problem are the fundamental questions of the meaning of the concept of mental retardation. That mental retardation is more complex than revealed by a low score on an individual test of intelligence is axiomatic. Yet just what is meant by subaverage mental development is not clear from current literature. Attempts, for example, to develop mathematical and mechanical models which simulate brain functions have been unsuccessful in regard to the functions of intellectual divergence and evaluation. These associational, reorganizational, and inventive activities have remained unduplicated in models. Model theory, therefore, does not seem to hold much immediate promise in the delineation of the dimensions of mental subnormality—for providing axiomatic statement of the nature of mental subnormality.

The problem then becomes one of specifying the vast array of behaviors which are concomitants of mental subnormality. This calls for the defining of mental subnormality in behavioristic terms. Unfortunately such a task becomes enormously complex because the criteria must be sequential and therefore situationally contaminated.

The American Association on Mental Deficiency, for example, has referred to subaverage mental development which manifests itself in the inability of the individual to adapt to the demands of the environment.[5] Among young children, this shows as a slow rate of maturation. The school-age children are unable to adapt to the demands of the learning environment of the school. The older mentally subnormal youngsters must adapt to the demands of independent living and work performance. Thus appropriate adaptive behavior becomes the guide to suspected mental subnormality. If a person at whatever age does not manifest appropriate adaptive behavior but shows a "normal" intelligence test performance, he is *not* considered mentally subnormal. Thus the criterion of lack of adaptive behavior *and* a low intelligence test score must both be identified in the determination of mental subnormality. Yet an individual who does show appropriate adaptive behavior but who scores low on an individual test of intelligence is considered mentally subnormal. The inconsistency of this definitional approach has been commented upon in Chapter 1. Unfortunately no appropriate alternatives have been worked out. Low intelligence test performance is the only factor which is common to the classification—yet the behavior of the mentally subnormal is infinitely more variable than is suggested by a low score on an intelligence test.

The problem has the additional complexities which derive from attempts to classify the mentally subnormal into categories which have greater homogeneity. Etiological classifications do not provide for degrees of subnormality. Educational classifications are suspect because they have been extended (incorrectly) to provide vocational prediction. Educability, for example, presumably implies potential for independent or semi-independent living and vocational skills given proper training. But the classification of educability is typically assigned from I.Q. scores (50 to about 85). Thus intelligence test scores which have fair predictive characteristics for educational success are called upon to predict vocational success. Certainly more comprehensive behavior criteria are needed for the determination of subnormal mental functioning if this condition is to be considered in its relationship to employment.

It seems somewhat ironic that prediction is attempted at all in this field. Given an individual who has deficient mental equipment to begin with, the predictions are then made to sequential criteria, nearly all of which are contaminated by either difficult to specify work or environmental conditions. For example, at the level of unskilled labor, there is no classification of jobs by level of complexity. Jobs may have an almost infinite variety of demands: speed, strength, co-ordination, judgment, foresight and pressure, yet all be classified as unskilled. Each of the peculiar demands of a job may be critical to its successful performance. At present, however, it is impossible to specify job complexity as a criterion for prediction because this information is simply not available.

A second area of concern is supervision. A given individual

may or may not be successful on a particular job depending upon the nature of the supervision provided: benign, oppressive, supportive or laissez-faire. An accurate and valid method of classifying supervision has not been developed.

A third problem is that of employee-employee relationships. For example, a person's behavior could be considered acceptable if he interacts appropriately with his fellow workers. On the other hand, it could be considered acceptable if he had no interaction with his fellow workers. He might also be tolerated as a scapegoat for their aggressions. This suggests that interfering behavior is the critical element in these relationships. Yet what constitutes interfering behavior under what circumstances? Slowdowns, mistakes, and poor procedures could be interpreted as interfering; so could talking, singing, asking questions, and physical contact such as pushing. Until acceptable behavior is specified, predicting success will be most difficult.

In the independent living area conditions of precisely what elements are critical need clarification. Dimensions of family support, acceptable leisure time activities, and degrees of independent behavior are frequently mentioned but seldom specified.

Research workers have attempted to predict future vocational success from present observations of a person in a controlled environment or from tests. The extent of retardation is unspecified, the conditions of work and performance demands are not specified and the conditions of living or support are unknown. Even the operational definition of successful employment is not agreed on. Must one get and hold a job for a specified period of time or is it better to judge success relative to the per cent of available work time a person is employed regardless of the number of different jobs held?

It appears that a working definition of employment success is needed first. With this agreed upon definition, it then appears most feasible to predict for two criteria: work performance and independent living. Thus it may be necessary to specify that a given individual has the skills to perform certain kinds of tasks under certain conditions of work under a certain kind of supervision with co-workers who treat him in a certain manner. Then attention can be turned to those conditions which must be supplied him to allow for a particular degree of independent living. At best this could lead to only tenuous prediction: such as to say the chances are one in three that a particular person will be successful on a job which has certain kinds of work requirements—given a particular kind of supervision on the job and the presence of certain conditions in his personal living environment.

This calls for a complete shift in approach. It requires first, the identification of a large group of adult individuals who can be designated as mentally subnormal. Second, agreement on what is "successful" employment must then be reached. Third, three groups of individuals must be specified: successful, marginally successful, and unsuccessful. The three groups can then be intensively studied to determine their vocational skills and their intellectual, personal, and social characteristics. Then the jobs they have been performing need thorough investigation to assess the major requirements for successful performance, the conditions of the jobs, and the type of supervision. If this procedure is followed for all three groups, degrees of failure as well as success can be specified. Finally, the living conditions of the three groups need to be examined to determine precise factors in the environment which are supportive and which are not.

With this data, it would be comforting to believe that a huge matrix could then be developed and the magic of factor analysis would indicate the dimensions of success. Even with this array of information, it is probable that employability is a highly specific thing for any given person, but the precision of a "The chances are . . ." statement could be measurably improved. Perhaps, since this is the area of human prediction, the best that can be expected is a rather sizeable range of imperfection. The researcher can then concentrate on narrowing the range, not developing precise predictive formulae. A dividend which might be expected from this procedure could be the development of quite radically different methods of training. This, in turn, would distort the original information gathered thus precipitating a whole new cycle of investigations. Researchers, at least, would not be in immediate danger of unemployment.

Of greater significance is the very good possibility that the concept of mental subnormality would be clarified. Any construct is useful to the degree that it accurately describes characteristics which are identified in the world of reality. To say that the only link of the concept of mental subnormality to the world of reality is a low score on a test of intelligence is obviously a gross oversimplification of the concept. Any person who has worked with the mentally subnormal is cognizant of the great diversity in behavior, looks, and ability represented. The concept must account for this diversity in a precise, specific, and exclusive manner if it is to have any scientific usefulness.

Investigators being what they are, it seems likely that the practical problems associated with the vocational development of the mentally subnormal will continue to intrigue researchers. It would seem more profitable, however, to plan a strategic attack to develop a better understanding of the concept of mental subnormality. With this approach, both immediate and long-range, practical, and basic questions have a greater chance of being investigated in a systematic and meaningful manner. The beneficiaries would be the yet unborn generations of youngsters who may not suffer quite so much from the consequences of inadequate mental development because the world is somewhat more able to provide opoprtunities which make their disability less penalizing for them than for former generations.

APPENDICES / NOTES / INDEX

APPENDIX **A**

SUGGESTED DAILY SCHEDULES

Freshman Year: Classroom and Prevocational Evaluation Schedule

Period	Time	Classes	Unit Credit
1	8:10–8:25	Homeroom	—
2	8:32–9:22	Physical Education and Health	¼
3	9:39–10:29	Reading (Language Arts)	1
4	10:36–11:26	Mathematics	1
5	11:30–11:58	Social Studies	1
	11:58–12:23	Lunch Period	—
	12:23–12:48	Vocational Information	¼
6	12:55–1:45	Vocational Information (continued)	¼
7	1:52–2:42	Prevocational Evaluation	¼
8	2:49–3:39	Prevocational Evaluation (continued	¼
		Total Unit Credits	4¼

Sophomore and Junior Years: Classroom and Job Tryout or Vocational Adjustment Training Schedule

Period	Time	Classes	Unit Credit
1	8:10–8:25	Homeroom	—
2	8:32–9:22	Physical Education and Health	¼
3	9:39–10:29	Language Arts and/or Reading	1
4	10:36–11:26	Mathematics	1
5	11:33–11:58	Social Studies or Vocational Orientation	1
	11:58–12:23	Lunch Period	—

Period	Time	Classes	Unit Credit
	12:23–12:48	Vocational Adjustment or Job Tryout	¼
6	12:55–1:45	Vocational Adjustment (continued)	¼
7	1:52–2:42	Vocational Adjustment (continued	¼
8	2:49–3:39	Vocational Adjustment (continued)	¼
		Total Unit Credits	4¼

Senior Year: Classroom and Vocational Training Schedule

Period	Time	Classes	Unit Credit
1	8:10–8:25	Homeroom	—
2	8:32–9:22	Physical Education and Health	¼
3	9:39–10:29	(Continued Remedial or Advanced Courses)	1
4	10:36–11:26	(Continued Remedial or Advanced Courses)	1
5	11:33–11:58	Supervised Vocational Placement	2
	11:58–12:23	Lunch Period	—
	12:23–12:48	Supervised Vocational Placement (continued)	—
6	12:55–1:45	Supervised Vocational Placement (continued)	—
7	1:52–2:42	Supervised Vocational Placement (continued)	—
8	2:49–3:39	Supervised Vocational Placement (continued)	—
		Total Unit Credits	4¼

EMPLOYER'S PROGRESS REPORT*

Student's name _____ Job no. _____

Employer's name _____ Address _____

Date started _____ Date completed _____

Time spent on job _____ Job title _____

Supervisor _____

(Please place a check in the space provided that best describes the trainee's performance at the time of rating and indicate whether or not he is improving. This form is intended to rate the trainee's progress at the completion of the second week on each job. Please add any recommendations, comments, or factors that are pertinent.)

Attendance	Absent _____ Days _____ Reason _____ Tardy _____ Times _____ Reason _____
Attitude	_____ Good _____Fair _____Poor _____Improving _____ Not improving
Personal Habits **and Appearance**	_____ Good _____ Fair _____Poor _____ Improving _____Not improving
Social **Relationships**	_____ Good _____ Fair _____Poor _____ Improving _____Not improving
Initiative	_____ Good _____ Fair _____Poor _____ Improving _____Not improving
Perseverance	_____ Good _____ Fair _____Poor _____ Improving _____Not improving
Understanding	_____ Good _____ Fair _____Poor _____ Improving _____Not improving

* Taken from the Employment Evaluation and Training Project Vocational Adjustment Training, Southern Illinois University.

APPENDIX B

| Quality of Work | _____ Good | _____ Fair | _____Poor |
| | _____ Improving | _____Not improving | |

| Quantity of Work | _____ Good | _____ Fair | _____Poor |
| | _____ Improving | _____Not improving | |

In your judgment, does this trainee possess the potential to perform adequately this type of work? Yes _____ Questionable _____ No _____ If questionable or no, explain:

Recommendations and/or comments:

EMPLOYER'S EVALUATION REPORT*

Student's name _____ Job no. _____

Employer's name _____ Address _____

Date started _____ Date completed _____

Time spent on job _____ Job title _____

Supervisor _____

(Please place a check in the space provided that best describes this trainee's performance at the time of rating. This form is intended to evaluate and rate the trainee's performance and his potential for employment upon completion of each job. All comparisons are to be made with the average employee on this job. Please add any recommendations, comments, or factors that are pertinent.)

PERSONALITY AND SOCIAL ADJUSTMENT

Attitude	_____ Enthusiastic
	_____ Co-operative
	_____ Indifferent Explain _____
	_____ Not co-operative Explain _____

Personal Habits and Appearance	_____ Above average
	_____ Acceptable
	_____ Not acceptable Explain _____

Social Relationships	_____ Above average
	_____ Acceptable
	_____ Not acceptable Explain _____

Realistic Characteristics	Goals	Yes _____	No _____
	Plan or approach	Yes _____	No _____
	Seriousness of purpose	Yes _____	No _____
	Comment	_____	

Inter-personal Characteristics	Friendly	Yes _____	No _____
	Explain	_____	

* Taken from the Employment Evaluation and Training Project Vocational Adjustment Training, Southern Illinois University.

APPENDIX C

Self-confident	Yes _____	No _____
Explain _____		
Trustworthy	Yes _____	No _____
Explain _____		

	Accepts criticism	Yes _____	No _____
	Explain _____		
	Accepts authority	Yes _____	No _____
	Explain _____		
Frustration	Accepts pressure	Yes _____	No _____
Tolerance	Explain _____		
	Accepts handicap	Yes _____	No _____
	Explain _____		
	Accepts own inadequacies	Yes _____	No _____
	Explain _____		

WORK HABITS AND EFFICIENCY

Punctuality
_____ Above average
_____ Acceptable
_____ Not acceptable
Explain _____

Supervision

Amount required:	Type:	Reaction:
_____ constant	_____ authoritative	_____ accepts
_____ frequent	_____ supportive	_____ resists
_____ limited	_____ critical	
_____ none		

Comment _____

Initiative
_____ Interested and active
_____ Indifferent   Explain _____
_____ Disinterested and idle
Explain _____

Perseverance
_____ Completes work
_____ Requires prodding
_____ Gives up
Comment _____

Quality of Work	_____ Above average	
	_____ Adequate	
	_____ Not adequate	Explain _____

Quantity of Work	_____ Above average	
	_____ Adequate	
	_____ Not adequate	Explain _____

Understanding	_____ Learns tasks adequately Yes ___ No ___
	If no, explain _____
	Follows instructions Yes ___ No ___
	If no, explain _____

Problem Solving	Recognizes own errors Yes ___ No ___
	If recognized, corrects own errors
	Yes ___ No ___
	Comment _____

1. Does this trainee possess any physical handicap or disability?

    Yes _____   No _____

2. If so, does the handicap or disability interfere with his work?

    Yes _____   No _____

3. Did the trainee incur any injury while on this job?

    Yes _____   No _____

4. Describe any unusual condition (such as emotional problem, social inadequacy, personal habit, mental ability, etc.) which could or does affect this trainee's performance: _____

5. Has this trainee demonstrated progress in his performance on this job?

    Yes _____   No _____

    Describe and explain _____

6. Has this trainee demonstrated those abilities, such as physical and mechanical skills, reading and writing ability, and safety consciousness, to perform this job adequately?

    Yes _____   No _____

    Describe and explain _____

7. In your judgment, does this trainee possess the potential and qualifications necessary to succeed in this type of work?

    Yes _____ Questionable _____ No _____

    If questionable or no, explain _____

8. Would you be as willing to hire this individual as you would your average applicant, if a job were available?

    Yes _____ Probably _____ Probably not _____ No _____

    If the above answer is "Probably not" or "No," please answer the following:

    Would hire IF . . . (state conditions):

9. Recommendations and/or comments:

JOB ANALYSIS REPORT

1. Job title _____

2. Description of duties _____

_____

3. Tools needed _____

4. What kind of job is it?
  _____ clerical
  _____ sales
  _____ agriculture
  _____ service
  _____ self employed
  _____ factory

5. Job level
  _____ skilled
  _____ semiskilled
  _____ unskilled

6. Experience
  _____ required
  _____ no required

7. Employment
  _____ full time
  _____ part time
  _____ seasonal

8. How many people employed?
  _____ male
  _____ female

9. What tests are given?
  _____ employment service tests
  _____ company made test
  _____ other
  _____ none

10. What kinds of licenses are required?
  _____ driver's license

_____ health certificate

_____ other

11. Must the employee fill out a written application?

_____ yes   _____ no

12. Must the employee belong to a union?

_____ yes   _____ no

13. How are employees found?

_____ employment service

_____ help wanted ads

_____ labor unions

_____ people come in

_____ referral by friends

_____ other

14. Do you have plenty of workers available?

_____ shortage

_____ steady supply

_____ more than enough

15. How are employees paid?

_____ hourly

_____ weekly

_____ monthly

_____ piecework

16. Does the employee

_____ work alone

_____ work with others

17. What are the working conditions?

_____ inside   _____ outside

_____ wet   _____ dry

_____ noisy   _____ quiet

_____ dirty   _____ clean

_____ day work   _____ night work

_____ high places   _____ low places   _____ neither

18. Does this job require

_____ standing

_____ sitting

_____ both
_____ climbing
_____ lifting
_____ carrying
_____ moving about
_____ driving

19. How much education is required?
_____ no formal education
_____ little formal education
_____ elementary school completion
_____ some high school
_____ high school diploma

20. How much on the job training is given?
_____ none
_____ less than 6 weeks
_____ 6 weeks to 6 months
_____ apprenticeship

21. How much adjustment to change is required?
_____ none
_____ little
_____ some
_____ frequent

22. Is there much pressure on the job?
_____ none
_____ little
_____ some
_____ great

23. How much supervision is the employee given?
_____ none
_____ little
_____ some
_____ much

24. Does the employee handle money?
_____ yes
_____ no

25. How much memory is required?

_____ none

_____ little

_____ memory for oral directions

_____ much

26. Does the employee meet the public?

_____ none

_____ seen by public

_____ talks to public

_____ works with public all of the time

27. How much reading is required on the job?

_____ none

_____ little

_____ addresses

_____ sales orders

_____ patterns

_____ directions

_____ bulletins

_____ letters

28. How much arithmetic is required?

_____ none

_____ little

_____ counting

_____ adding

_____ subtracting

_____ multiplying

_____ dividing

_____ fractions

_____ measurements

_____ sales slips

_____ invoices

_____ other

29. How much writing is required?

_____ none

_____ listing

_____ production records

_____ sales orders

_____ information to be read by others

30. What kind of speaking is required?

_____ little

_____ giving messages

_____ asking for materials or tools

_____ giving directions

31. How much strength is required?

Hands:	_____ none	_____ little	_____ some	_____ great
Arms:	_____ none	_____ little	_____ some	_____ great
Legs:	_____ none	_____ little	_____ some	_____ great
Back:	_____ none	_____ little	_____ some	_____ great

NOTES

Chapter 1

1. J. M. Itard, *The Wild Boy of Aveyron* (New York: Century Company, 1932).
2. Edward Seguin, *Idiocy; And Its Treatment by the Physiological Method* (New York: Bureau of Publications, Teachers College, Columbia University, 1907).
3. Alfred Binet and Theodore Simon, *The Development of Intelligence in Children* (Baltimore: Williams and Wilkins, 1916).
4. Lee Joseph Cronbach, *Essentials of Psychological Testing* (New ed.; New York: Harper & Row).
5. Wayne Dennis, *Readings in the History of Psychology* (New ed.; New York: Appleton-Century-Crofts, 1948).
6. Edwin G. Boring, *A History of Experimental Psychology* (2nd ed.; New York: Appleton-Century-Crofts, 1950).
7. Lewis M. Terman and Maud A. Merrill, *Stanford-Binet Intelligence Scale* (Manual for the Third Revision, Form L–M) (Boston: Houghton Mifflin, 1960).
8. J. L. H. Down, "Observations on an Ethnic Classification of Idiocy," *Reports and Observations from the London Hospital,* III (1866), 259–62.
9. George A. Jervis, "Medical Aspects of Mental Deficiency," *Amer. Jour. of Mental Deficiency,* LVII (1952), 175–88.
10. Alfred A. Strauss and Laura E. Lehtinen, *Psychopathology and Education of the Brain-Injured Child* (New York: Grune and Stratton, 1947).
11. Alfred A. Strauss and Newell C. Kephart, *Psychopathology and Education of the Brain-Injured Child, Volume II: Progress in Theory and Clinic* (New York: Grune and Stratton, 1955).
12. Samuel A. Kirk and G. Orville Johnson, *Educating the Retarded Child* (Boston: Houghton Mifflin, 1951).
13. Rick F. Heber, "A Manual on Terminology and Classification in Mental Retardation," *Amer. Jour. of Mental Deficiency* (Monograph Supplement), LXIV (Sept., 1959).
14. Thomas E. Jordan, *The Exceptional Child* (Columbus, Ohio: Charles E. Merrill, 1962), pp. 150–52.

15. William M. Cruickshank and G. Orville Johnson (eds.), *Education of Exceptional Children and Youth* (Englewood Cliffs, N.J.: Prentice-Hall, 1958), p. 10.
16. Henry Herbert Goddard, *The Kallikak Family: A Study in the Heredity of Feeble-Mindedness* (New York: Macmillan, 1912).
17. Itard, *op. cit.*
18. Amelie Hamaide, *The Decroly Class* (New York: E. P. Dutton, 1924).
19. Alice Descoeudres, *The Education of Mentally Defective Children* (Boston: Heath, 1928).
20. Annie Dolman Inskeep, *Teaching Dull and Retarded Children* (New York: Macmillan, 1926).
21. John Spenser Duncan, *Education of the Ordinary Child* (New York: Ronald Press, 1943).
22. Christine Ingram, *Education of the Slow-Learning Child* (3rd ed.; New York: Ronald Press, 1960).
23. Kirk and Johnson, *op. cit.*
24. Herbert Goldstein and Dorothy Seigel, *A Curriculum Guide for Teachers of the Educable Mentally Handicapped*, Circular Series B–3, No. 12 (Springfield, Illinois: Superintendent of Public Instruction, 1958).
25. Godfrey Stevens, "An Analysis of the Objectives for the Education of Children With Retarded Mental Development," *Amer. Jour. of Mental Deficiency*, LXIII (Sept. 1958), 225–35.
26. B. J. House and D. Zeaman, "Visual Discrimination Learning in Imbeciles," *Amer. Jour. of Mental Deficiency*, LXIII (Nov., 1958), 447–52.
27. G. N. Cantor and J. V. Hottel, "Discrimination Learning in Mental Defectives as a Function of Magnitude of Food Reward and Intelligence Level," *Amer. Jour. of Mental Deficiency*, LX (Oct., 1955), 380–84.
28. Cf., Norman R. Ellis (ed.), *Handbook of Mental Deficiency* (New York: McGraw-Hill, 1963). This comprehensive discussion of psychological theory and research provides excellent presentations of differing points of view. It is noteworthy for diversity, not unity.
29. Cf., Herbert Goldstein, "Social and Occupational Adjustment," in Harvey A. Stevens and Rick Heber (eds.), *Mental Retardation, A Review of Research* (Chicago: University of Chicago Press, 1964). Also Ruby Jo Kennedy, *A Connecti-*

cut *Community Rvisited: A Study of the Social Adjustment of a Group of Mentally Deficient Adults in 1948 and
1960.* Project No. 65 (Office of Vocational Rehabilitation,
U.S. Department of Health, Education, and Welfare, Washington, D.C., June 30, 1962). A most interesting follow-up
comparison suggesting the consequences of mental retardation when social class is constant, provocative suggestions
for training programs.

Chapter 2

1. Elia Binzberg, "Development and Education," *The Nation's
   Children: Development and Education* (New York: Columbia University Press, 1960), p. 152.
2. Abraham Ribicoff, *Testimony for the Sub-Committee on Special Education.* Committee on Education and Labor. U.S.
   House of Representatives, Concerning H. S. 7178, July,
   1961.
3. Robert Havighurst and Lindley Stiles, "The National Policy
   for Alienated Youth," *Phi Delta Kappan,* XLII (April,
   1961), 284.
4. Paul Bowman and Charles Matthews, *Motivation of Youth for
   Leaving School.* Project 200, Cooperative Research Program, U.S. Office of Education. Sept., 1960.
5. James Bryant Conant, *The American High School Today*
   (New York: McGraw-Hill, 1959).
6. Ribicoff, *op. cit.*
7. W. R. Baller, "A Study of the Present Social Status of a
   Group of Adults, Who, When They Were in Elementary
   School, Were Classified as Mentally Deficient," *Genetic
   Psychological Monographs,* III (June, 1936), 165–244.
8. D. C. Charles, "Ability and Accomplishment of Persons Earlier
   Judged Mentally Deficient," *Genetic Psychological Monographs,* XLVII (February, 1953), 3–71.
9. Ruby Jo Kennedy, *The Social Adjustment of Morons in a
   Connecticut City* (Hartford, Connecticut: Southbury Training Schools, Social Service Department, 1948).
10. H. R. Phelps, "Postschool Adjustment of Mentally Retarded
    Children in Select Ohio Cities," *Exceptional Child,* XXIII
    (November, 1956), 58–62.
11. A. Channing, *Employment of Mentally Deficient Boys and*

Girls (Washington, D.C.: U.S. Children's Bureau Publication No. 219, 1932, p. 107).

12. N. Keys and J. M. Nathan, "Occupations for the Mentally Handicapped," *Jour. of Applied Psychology*, XVI (1932), 497–511.

13. D. Fryer, "Psychology in its Vocational Application: A Survey of Recent Literature," *Mental Hygiene*, XI (1927), 124–39.

14. C. S. Raymond, "Industrial Possibilities of the Feebleminded," *Industrial Psychology*, II (1927), 473–78.

15. Arthur L. Rautman, "Society's First Responsibility to the Mentally Retarded," *Amer. Jour. of Mental Deficiency*, LIV (1949), 155–62.

16. A. J. Shafter, "Criteria for Selecting Institutionalized Mental Defectives for Vocational Placement," *Amer. Jour. of Mental Deficiency*, LXI (1957), 599–616.

17. L. Cowan and M. Goldman, "Selection of the Mentally Deficient for Vocational Training and the Effect of this Training on Vocational Success," *Jour. of Consulting Psychology*, XXIII (1959), 78–84.

18. Walter S. Neff, "The Success of a Rehabilitation Program—A Follow-Up Study of Clients of the Vocational Adjustment Center," *Monographs, No. 3, The Jewish Vocational Service* (Chicago: *ca.* 1959).

19. M. C. Reynolds and C. L. Stunkard, *A Comparative Study of Day Class vs. Institutionalized Educable Retardates*, Project 192 (Minneapolis: College of Education, University of Minnesota, 1960).

20. Oliver P. Kolstoe, "The Employment Evaluation and Training Program," *Amer. Jour. of Mental Deficiency*, LXV (July 1960), 17–31.

21. Fount G. Warren, "Ratings of Employed and Unemployed Mentally Handicapped Males on Personality and Work Factors," *Amer. Jour. of Mental Deficiency*, LXV (March, 1961), 629–33.

22. Oliver P. Kolstoe, "An Examination of Some Characteristics Which Discriminate Between Employed and Not-Employed Mentally Retarded Males," *Amer. Jour. of Mental Deficiency*, LXVI (Nov. 1961), 472–82.

23. The writers are indebted to Mrs. Janice Holloway for the levels analysis performed by her.

24. Warren, *op. cit.*

25. Cf., Altoona Public School Program, Altoona, Pa. and Warren

C. Bower, *Adjustment of the Retarded,* A Report on Project No. 330–C (Washington: Office of Vocational Rehabilitation, U.S. Department of Health, Education, and Welfare, January, 1962).
26. Kirk and Johnson, *op. cit.*

Chapter 3

1. Oliver P. Kolstoe, "A Comparison of Mental Abilities of Bright and Dull Children of Comparable Mental Ages," *Jour. of Educ. Psychology,* XLV (March, 1954), 161–68.
2. Lloyd M. Dunn and Rudolph J. Capobianco, "Mental Retardation: A Review of Research," *Rev. of Educ. Research,* XXIX (December, 1959), 451–70.
3. Marion White McPherson, "Learning and Mental Deficiency," *Amer. Jour. of Mental Deficiency,* LXII (March, 1958), 870–77.
4. Donald J. Stedman, "Associative Clustering of Semantic Categories in Normal and Retarded Subjects," *Amer. Jour. of Mental Deficiency,* LXVII (March, 1963), 700–704.
5. Samuel A. Kirk, *Educating Exceptional Children* (Boston: Houghton Mifflin, 1962), p. 110.
6. C. L. Stacey and M. De Martino, *Counseling and Psychotherapy with the Mentally Retarded* (Glencoe, Ill.: Free Press, 1958).
7. A. H. Maslow, *Motivation and Personality* (New York: Harper, 1954).
8. William H. Burton, "Basic Principles in a Good Teaching-Learning Situation," *Readings in Human Learning,* eds. Lester D. Crow and Alice Crow (New York: David McKay, 1963), pp. 7–19.
9. M. Beekman, "Lansing, Michigan," *Preparation of Mentally Retarded Youth for Gainful Employment,* U.S. Department of Health, Education, and Welfare Bulletin No. 28 (Washington: U.S. Government Printing Office, 1959), p. 59.

Chapter 4

1. R. L. Erdman, "Vocational Choices of Adolescent Mentally Retarded Boys." (Unpublished Doctor's Dissertation, University of Illinois, 1957).
2. Beekman, *op. cit.*

3. Charles Eskridge, *The Texas Plan for Rehabilitation of Mentally Retarded and Severely Physically Handicapped through a Cooperative Program between the Division of Vocational Rehabilitation, Special Education, and Independent School Districts.*
4. *Kent County Program* (Grand Rapids, Mich.: Kent County Department of Special Education).
5. In this connection, two surveys made in 1962 are of interest. Juanita Neunlist surveyed the city of West Frankfort, Illinois, a town of less than 10,000 population, where some 1200 workers were rendered unemployed by the closing of railroad shops. Despite the great problem of unemployment, she found 24 jobs which could be done by and were available to mentally retarded children.

   Mary Cosby surveyed Metropolis, Illinois, a city of 7,300. She found 298 positions which could be filled by the mentally retarded. Job placement in businesses which are engaged in interstate commerce require a specific certificate from the U.S. Dept. of Labor to meet the requirements of the Fair Labor Practices Act.

Chapter 5

1. Kennedy, Phelps, Baller, Charles, *op. cit.*
2. The writers are indebted to Mr. John Morton and Mr. Joseph Fransic, special class teachers in the Kent County Michigan program for recommending the following materials which have usable sections for teaching the academic aspects of the program.
   a) Charles H. Kahn and J. Bradley Hanna, *Using Dollars and Sense* (San Francisco: Fearon Publishers, Inc., 1961). This is a simplified introduction to money.
   b) Esther O. Carson and Flora M. Daly, *Teen-Agers Prepare for Work* (Esther O. Carson, 18623 Lake Chabot Road, Castro Valley, Calif., $1.95).

      Book I discusses factory workers, messenger service, food service, dishwashing, babysitting, gasoline station, and has stories, work sheets, spelling, and activities.

      Book II discusses self analysis, work experience, getting a job, holding a job, spending the income, has stories, work sheets, spelling and activities.
   c) Lawson, Gary D., *Everyday Business* (Sacramento, Calif.:

Pierson Trading Company, 1958). Order from Gary D. Lawson, Rt. 2, Box 2804, Elk Grove, Calif., $1.60. This book deals with banking, budgeting, buying, federal income tax, insurance, activity sheets.

d) *Learning and Writing English.* Books I and II (Austin, Texas: The Steck Co., 1950). Has exercises in basic writing and English, and is written for foreign born.

e) Herman Goldberg and Winifred Brumber, eds., *Rochester Occupational Education Series* (Chicago: Science Research Associates, 1963). Has stories and activities.

f) *Skill Builders* (Pleasantville, N.Y.: Readers Digest, Educ. Division) Grade 2, 3, 4, 5, & 6: $25 per set.

g) "Target Series," *Employment I, Citizenship II, Family Living—Business Phase III* (Mafex Associates, Box 114, Ebensburg, Pa.). Contains student text, activities books, teacher's guides, posters: From $2.85 to $5.85.

h) Telephone books—people, places, stores, products, transportation used for identifying.

i) Altoona School District, *Occupational Education in the Altoona Senior High School,* Secondary Curriculum Series, Special Education. (Academic Units, Evaluation of Student, Work Experience program, including job training, student supervision and evaluation, remuneration, employer liability, possible problem situations.) Research results relative to program effectiveness. Suggestions to other school districts. Forms currently used in occupational education, high school sequence for graduation, parental consent for work experience, employer's rating form, employer's guide for writing letter of recommendation, facsimile of certificate of attainment, 1962. ($2.00).

j) Margaret A. Neuber, *Social Skills for Living and Learning: A Guide for Teachers of Children with Retarded Mental Development* (University Park, Pa.: Pennsylvania State University Special Education Workshop, 1959). The contents include: Children's Workshop—The Primary Group; Children's Workshop—The Intermediate Group; Occupational or Job Exploratory Education—Junior High School—the world of work, survey of school job training opportunities, readiness for employability, on the job training; home making and family living; family membership, growing up, teen-age responsibilities, managing time, first aid, child study, baby sitting, community membership—work areas, government, health, recreation, growth and development; Occupational or job exploratory education—Senior High School—the world of work, you and your job, on the job training, samples of suggested forms; home making and family living, looking toward marriage, budgeting and managing income, planning a home, family health, child care, managing time; citizenship, basis of citizenship, broadening and understanding.

3. Roger M. Frey and Dan S. Rainey, "The Utility of Commercially Produced Programmed Instruction with Educable Mentally Retarded Children" (Unpublished, 1963).

4. The writers are indebted to Neil MacGregor for examples of lesson materials in this section.

5. Cowan and Goldman, *op. cit.*

6. Neff, *op. cit.*

Chapter 6

1. The writers are indebted to Mr. and Mrs. Vincent P. Farrell for much of the information in this section.

2. Fount G. Warren, "Kent County Occupational and Educational Training Project, Progress Report," 1963.

3. The writers wish to thank Dr. Martin B. Loeb, Professor of Social Work, The University of Wisconsin for suggesting the relationship between economic approaches and rehabilitation of the handicapped which eventuated in the discussion on sheltered workshops and economic positions. (speech, Nov. 3, 1963).

4. The National Association of Sheltered Workshops and Homebound Programs, 1029 Vermont Avenue N.W., Suite 1102, Washington 5, D.C., has pamphlets which are specifically written to explain different aspects of workshop operations.

5. A summary of practices in contract procurement is presented in Michael M. Dalnick, *Contract Procurement Practices of Sheltered Workshops* (National Society for Crippled Children and Adults, Inc., 2023 W. Ogden Ave., Chicago, Ill. 1963).

6. For example, the Diagraph-Bradley Company of Herrin, Illinois manufactures stencil supplies for commercial firms. One product is a special ink. Filling the ink cans, labeling and packaging is considered a "messy" job by the employees. The company and the workers were very happy to sub-

contract this job to the Employment Training Center. This led to a deep and abiding interest in the problems of the handicapped by the president of Diagraph-Bradley, the late J. W. Brigham.

Chapter 7

1. Heber, *op. cit.*
2. Itard, *op. cit.*
3. Seguin, *op. cit.*
4. Samuel A. Kirk, *Early Education of the Mentally Retarded; an Experimental Study* (Urbana: Univ. of Illinois Press, 1958).
5. Heber, *op. cit.*

INDEX

Academic work. *See* Arithmetic; Reading
Alms houses, 5
Altoona Public School Program, 168n
Altoona School District, 171n
American Association on Mental Deficiency: committee on nomenclature, 15; mentioned, 23, 143
Arithmetic: prevocational, 100–102; job tryout, 102–3; permanent placement, 103
Attention span, 51
Axioms. *See* Curriculum

Baller, W. R., 34, 91, 167n, 170n
Beekman, M., 169n, 170n
Binet, Alfred; defining intelligence, 9, 165n
Binzberg, Elia, 28, 167n
Boring, Edwin G., 165n
Bower, Warren C., 169n
Bowman, Paul, 28, 167n
Brigham, J. W., 173n
British Royal Commission for the Feebleminded, 10, 11
Brumber, Winifred, 171n
Burton, William H., 55, 169n

California: sheltered workshops, 113
California Test of Achievement, 37
Cantor, G. N., 23, 166n
Capobianco, Rudolph J., 51, 169n
Carson, Esther O., 170n
Channing, A., 34, 168n
Charles, D. C., 91, 167n, 170n
Classroom: space requirements, 66–67; facilities needed, 66–67
Conant, James Bryant, 28, 167n
Cosby, Mary, 170n
Counseling: theory, 51; of parents, 110–11; mentioned, 76, 77

Cowan, L., 35, 110, 168n, 172n
Cronbach, Lee Joseph, 9, 165n
Crow, Alice, 169n
Crow, Lester D., 169n
Cruickshank, William M., 166n
Curricula: early, 17–19; dumping grounds, 19; relief, 19–20; changing public school emphasis, 19–23; crafts, 20; happiness, 20; remedial-academic, 20–21
Curriculum: guides, 21–22; need for different kind, 29; empirical base, 34–49; components of, 47–48; historical perspective, 50; from research, 50; from learning characteristics, 50–52; and intelligence, 56; and personal appearance, 56–57; social developments, 57–58; vocational skills, 58–59; in workshops, 124–25

Dalnick, Michael M., 172n
Daly, Flora M., 170n
Deaf and dumb, 16
Decroly, O., 18
De Martino, M., 51, 169n
Dennis, Wayne, 9, 165n
Descoeudres, Alice, 18, 166n
Diagraph Bradley Company, 173n
Differential Aptitude Test, 37
Disability: attitude towards, 3; and political philosophy, 3; treatment of, 3–7
Division of Vocational Rehabilitation: Illinois, 36; Texas, 85
Down, J. L. H., 13, 165n
Driver training, 94, 95
Dunn, Lloyd M., 51, 169n
Duncan, John Spenser, 18, 166n

Educable mentally retarded: defined, 14–15; mentioned, 29
Educational adjustment: regular class placement, 26; remedial programs, 27; track system, 27;

INDEX